The B

The White Guilt Messiah Complex, Democrats and Black Victims

By
Unpopular Politics

Table Of Contents

Introduction

W hy does the Democrat Party and the left in general speak so ill of the country? It's as though they are always trying to out do each other in some kind of top this ridiculous statement competition. It's either that, or a let's see who can show more contempt for the country challenge.

It is to the point that chanting U.S.A., U.S.A. is now considered as an act of white supremacy. Patriotism and love of country are now deemed as hyper-racism. Voicing that we should strive to achieve the dream of being a colorless society is white privilege. If a person says let's make America great again then it is a sure sign that person hates black people and people of color. Even Thanksgiving is now regarded by the left as an ode to white oppression.

Despising the country is now the hipster thing to do. The more you hate America the cooler you are. It is one of the most baffling things to behold.

We can thank the Democrat Party, the dishonest media, and the radical violent left for all of this. It did not all happen overnight. It happened via a very purposeful slow creep. Now here we are after decades working their plan.

All of a sudden, after doing the grueling work necessary as a country to make a society that provides opportunity for all, the goal posts have shifted. The left now demands equality of outcome for all endeavors. Anything less is viewed as systemic racist subjugation.

Over the last few years the left has taken their radicalism to another level. They have shifted into overdrive. In the past they were content to hide their evil intentions. Today, they are emboldened. They are in control of the narrative, and they openly flaunt their disdain for the country. They publicly declare that they wish to tear down the whole system and transform it into their idea of a socialist utopia.

It is not far fetched to think that the left is desirous of inciting a race war. It sounds crazy, but when you compare their rhetoric that America hates all things non-white, with the country that America is in reality, it is time to more aggressively combat their evil intentions. The constant drum beat of racism suggests that something more insidious is at play.

This book attempts to point out how the left uses the race horse to disrupt American society and create an atmosphere of racist panic and hysteria. It is a series of commentary based on observations the author has made over many years after immigrating to the United States 26 years ago, but particularly in the last five years.

The author's desire is to help Americans who do not wish to continue going down this perilous road see the nefarious plans of the left, the media and the Democrat Party. Hopefully more people will get off the sidelines and get in the fight to defeat this nefarious machine.

Chapter 1

White Guilt
❖⊪————•••————⊪❖

Y. T. McWhitey Speaks (and you better listen)

Hi, my name is Y. T. McWhitey. Friends and enemies alike call me Y. T. I have a confession to make. I have white privilege! Not because there is anything special about me or anything. Given the color of my skin it's a no brainer that I have white privilege. But of course you already knew that. I am white after all. Ahh…it feels so liberating to say that. It's kind of strange…it also gives me a feeling of…of…of virtue…a feeling of…superiority even.

I know what you are thinking. As a white person, I need to be careful about feelings of superiority. After all did I not just confess that I have white privilege…a touch of racism even? You don't understand. I feel superior to other white people who do not understand their own white privilege and racist tendencies. That's the difference!

This puts me in a unique position to lecture fellow white people, while gaining browning poin…uh…credibility in the black community. Whenever I get the opportunity, I love to point out the racism of other white racists, who loves to hate, hate, hate.

There have been times when my confrere white brethren have protested and told me they are not racists. They point to the way they actually treat people as evidence that they are not racist. That is when I point out to them that it does not matter how they treat people. They must be aware of their unconscious racism. That is when they get really confused.

All that nonsense spoken by the revered Dr. Martin Luther King about judging people by the content of their character does not apply to white people. White people must be assessed as a group.

Let me give you an example of how white privilege works. One time, a black colleague and a white colleague of mine were arguing about something none work related. My white colleague got so frustrated with our black colleague that he told him he is ignorant and needs to shut up. I had to step in and remind my white colleague that as a privileged white male he should not be calling people of color ignorant. Nor should he tell them to shut up. Who was he to deny that black man his truth? To be honest that black colleague is a real jerk. Half the time he opens his mouth he really does not know what the heck he is talking about. However, that is beside the point. Because we possess white privilege we cannot treat black people as equals. They must be treated with kids gloves.

In another instance, I had to explain to a young white executive how white privilege works. He was telling me how hard he worked and how much he sacrificed to get where he is.

That was when I, Y. T. McWhitey had to bring him down a notch by explaining to him that he should not feel to proud of his so called "accomplishments."

You see, his great, great, great, great, great, great grandfather once owned slaves. As a descendant of these evil slave owners, it did not matter that he had to work two jobs, survive on a diet of Ramen Noodles, and struggle to pay his rent while he was in college. The many nights he spent burning the midnight oil studying hard had very little to do with his success in life. He needed to understand that he was the recipient of white privilege. It was my privilege…(heh heh, get it? Privilege!) to let him know.

White people also need to understand that it is never ok to laugh at people of color…ok? It does not matter how funny you might think it is. It…is…not…cool! One more time, as a white person, you do not make fun of people of color.

One time I had to pull my BFF aside and chastise him for laughing at a black man's hair style. True, it was a god awful hair style that made the black dude look like he was straight out of a 1860s circus side show, but that's his culture. It really upset me to see how insensitive my BFF could be, but I let him know. It was not ok. No one has the right to chuckle at that, especially a privileged white male.

I do this from a pure heart, and besides it also helps to keep unfavorable attention away from me…but that's not why I do it…really.

Sometimes I even have to speak truth to black people who do not understand how white privilege works. I have no problem telling black people who do not think the way that I do that they are race traitors.

They have to understand that nothing is ever their own fault…whatever the problem may be. It is my job to let black people know that the bank loans they have been denied, the police stops, the disparate incarceration rate, and every other problem they face in society is never their fault. It is the system's fault. They have to understand this. It is for their own good.

Any black person who does not accept this way of thinking, thinks differently, and has an independent mind is just an Uncle Tom who lives in the sunken place. They must understand that they are victims of the system and they need me, Y. T. McWhitey, to be their hero.

Don't you just love me?

The White Self Loathing Liberal Saboteur

The white liberal who is always involved in virtue signaling is a fool. This person wants desperately to be patted on the shoulder. Therefore, s/he engages in self sabotage, constantly punching himself/herself in his/her own face, screaming, begging for attention hoping that someone, anyone would recognize his/her "selflessness." This white lefty views his self-flagellation as heroic behavior, and craves attention from "people of color" especially black people. S/he wants to be their hero.

If that means castigating other white people for no other reason than them being white s/he is fully committed to that cause. This self-hating white liberal is easy to spot. S/he is the one who shouts the loudest, with a look of self satisfaction in a protest, with black people all around her. Down with white privilege   s/he screams with a look of pomposity on his/her face.

This self-saboteur wears a cloak of sanctimony that makes her feel a tingle run down her spine, because in her own mind she is demonstrating to the world that she cares. She is down with the struggle. She is happy to show up at rallies shouting f*** white supremacy at anyone who does not share her views.

It is wholly lost on this individual that at real white supremacy gatherings, the reason that the white supremacists are usually outnumbered ten fold by counter protesters is because most people are against that type of bigotry. Calling other white people racist with nothing to back it up is a favorite past time of this dolt because in his mind, it makes him look like he is sensitive and enlightened. He is woke doggone it! And he wants everyone to know it.

This fool, in her eagerness to demonstrate that she is one of the good white people thinks that it is a virtue to hold black people and others she has relegated to the realm of victims to a lower standard. The self-loathing white liberal thinks that it is his job to protect anyone who is not white. He will make excuses for bad behavior by them, even when the facts are slapping him in the face.

This white leftist loves getting that self congratulatory slap on the back as he shows the world that he is one of the mindful whites. Encouraged by the attention he craves, and receives for acting like he hates those who look like himself, he becomes more vociferous as he preaches about the dangers of old white men in particular, and the white male patriarchy in general.

At times he even calls for violence against those who look like himself, and he is often cheered on for being "brave." This white liberal saboteur says things like "without white boys being able to empathize with other people, humanity will continue to destroy itself." They say "I am ashamed to be white," or that the white nuclear family is promoting white supremacy. The white saboteur is filled with pride when he hears a prominent black person say "I have given up on white people." He nods his head in approval.

His presence is ubiquitous. She thrives on college campuses. She is in the class room indoctrinating those she has been charged to educate. She is poisoning young fertile minds devoid of the capacity to reason. He is on the student council demanding safe spaces for the easily offended. When he is not occupied securing safe spaces, he is making demands that anyone who disagrees with him not be allowed to speak on the campus. Delicate flower that he is, he has no problem throwing a tantrum when his indoctrinators fail to meet his demands. He excels at hurling insults and personal attacks at anyone he deems unworthy of a platform.

This white liberal is not averse to looting, rioting, and using violence as a tool. These "freedom fighters" are more dangerous than the Klu Klux Klan because unlike the Klu Klux Klan, whose numbers are few, and who lack power; they are many, many more. The media cheers them on and Hollywood loves them.

This white liberal saboteur hates independent black thinkers and other minorities who think for themselves. These white vainglorious social justice warriors save some of their most poisonous venom for independent thinking black people. In spectacular displays that demonstrate lack of self awareness, they often call the black independent thinker a race traitor, and accuse him of self loathing. These white liberals, so filled with virtue, and who want so much for the world to love them, and know that they are woke, have even been known to label some of their black detractors as "black white supremacists." They mean well, these buffoons. They are just trying to help. This, more than anything is what makes them dangerous

Beware The White Self Righteous Liberal And His Moral Preening

Below is a quote from Michael Moore:

"Two-thirds of all white guys voted for Trump." He continued, "That means anytime you see three white guys walking at you, down the street toward you, two of them voted for Trump. You need to move over to the other sidewalk because these are not good people that are walking toward you. You should be afraid of them."

Moore thinks that he is woke because he talks this way about the ethnic group to which he belongs, but this is dangerous rhetoric. Michael Moore thinks that because he has a poor opinion of Trump...which he is entitled to have by the way, that all White people should have the same opinion of Trump.

Donald Trump has never said or done anything that is so terrible that it demands people everywhere treat him like the plague. Trump has said uncomfortable things. He has said unpopular things. He has been uncouth and on occasion he has even been a jerk, but the idea that Trump is such a monster that people who vote for him are also monsters is ludicrous.

The idea that a certain race of people must reject Trump because some members of that race do not like him, and have a low opinion of him is the kind of thinking that continues to keep this country divided. Michael Moore is a dangerous man because he thinks it is a virtue to judge people by the color of their skin, and not the content of their character.

He is willing to deem tens of millions of Americans as villains because they voted for a man who wants low taxes, to control the borders, confront China on trade, and move the American Embassy to Jerusalem. Michael Moore thinks that if you are white you are supposed to love socialism, an ideology that we have proof has failed and caused death and misery everywhere it has been tried.

In Michael Moore's world view, if you are white and you support the changes Trump promised to bring to the VA, then you are an awful Human being. These changes have improved the life of veterans. If you support the right to try policy initiated by Trump for sick patients, then you are a bad whitey. If you are a caucasian who is against the radical transgender agenda, if you support the second amendment, or stand apologetically for the first amendment, then a person should walk to the other side of the street if approaching three of you on the street.

This is the kind of nonsense that passes for wokeness. People hearing this drivel should be in awe because it is such forward thinking. Really?!? The truth is that this is nothing more than moral self-aggrandizement. This is supposed to show that even though all of these evil white people voted for Trump, I Michael Moore am not one of them. I am enlightened!

It is also meant to pander to black people by encouraging them to have a negative attitude towards white people, not based on the content of these white people's character, but because Michael Moore thinks all white people should have the same opinion of Donald Trump.

Hidden in this backward way of thinking is the dirty little secret that Michael Moore believes all black people should feel the same way about Donald Trump the way that he Moore does. As long as they do, he considers them as good blacks. He even gets to pat himself on the shoulder and present himself as some kind of hero to the black man. That way, Moore gets a pass and escapes any scrutiny of his life because he is one of the good whiteys.

Do not doubt it for a moment. The white liberal like Michael Moore is a dangerous fellow.

White Lefties Just Keep on Fiddling

It is quite ironic observing woke white leftists play black people for fools, for absolute fools in the name of standing up for blacks. These white lefties portray black people en masse as some of the most foolish, weakest, most incapable, mindless people in America.

What perhaps is even more crazy is the way so many black people willingly play along with this non sense. So many black people just lap it up like it's water in a desert land. They are totally unconcerned that they are being played by the most dangerous group to black Americans.

This group of white lefties and a self appointed group of black Marxist agitator elites have convinced many black people that victimhood makes black people special. It is something to be attained, and blacks can be proud that victimology makes them special.

It is unbelievable watching the number of black people who continue to say no to the freedom that awaits them by casting off the chains that they so eagerly use to tie themselves down. These chains have been given to them by these white lefties who do not have one picogram of black people's interest at heart.

In fact, these white lefties care so little about black people that they are actively working on replacing blacks by importing a whole new underclass of people. This new underclass is to take the place of blacks, should black people ever get an awakening and cast off the chains that keep too many of them in mental bondage.

That is part of the reason Democrats are importing so many illegal immigrants from south and Central America into the country illegally. Doubt that? Look at the way that the numbers of black citizens have remained almost stagnant, as their numbers are surpassed through illegal immigration (but that's another topic for another time).

Despite all of this, so many black people continue to be enthralled by this victim mentality in a country where they can literally do anything, with so many tools available to them.

Any fellow black person who says that black people are not victims in America, that blacks are not persecuted and under siege is called a sell out and an Uncle Tom. The black victim class would rather walk around with the mental chains given to them by their white lefty saviors, and black elite power players. Too large a number of black people have no problem pretending to be oppressed. They latch on to the lies fed to them day after day by these white lefties and black power players.

Apart from the uselessness of this approach to life, there is a stunning lack of appreciation and a sense of ungratefulness for how blessed black people in America are in 2021. Why anyone or any group of people would choose such a pessimistic approach to life is beyond the imagination to provide. Maybe it's because that way people can always make excuses for failure. "It's not my fault, it's the system's fault."

Barrack Obama, Oprah Winfrey, Michael Eric Dyson, Marc Lamont Hill, Al Sharpton, Benjamin Krump, and other successful charlatans who peddle in black grievance are their gold standard.

Marcellus Wiley captured some amazing perspective and said it best. These charlatans would rather "tell black people that the odds are against them instead of telling them how to overcome the odds."

"They'd rather learn the names of George Floyd, Daunte Wright and Michael Brown," as a way to further burnish the victim mentality that they are oppressed. They are not inspired or interested in even learning the perspectives of men like Thomas Sowell, Shelby Steele, Allen West, Ben Carson, Coleman Hughes and others who defy the narrative.

It's time to end this. Black people, stop dancing as these white lefties who have no real interest in your welfare continue to fiddle, laughing at you while they play.

The Racism Wolf: The Politics of, and the Weaponization of Race

Is it possible that a white person may be a jerk to a black person without the white person being a racist? Is it just a handful of people who are just so sick and tired of the constant appeal to race in this country, where every single offensive thing that a white person does against a black person is immediately chalked down to racism? This is ridiculous!

No matter what the offense is, no matter the circumstances under which it happens, the cry is immediately RACISM. They then begin the mission to defame people's character and destroy their good name immediately. Sometimes an offense may legitimately be racially tinged, but it does not automatically make the person a racist.

People sometimes say things to cause pain because they feel hurt by something someone may have said or done. Human beings are flawed. They lie, they cheat, they steal, they kill and they commit all different appalling acts for many different reasons. Human beings are imperfect, but the way that they live their lives is important. They should be judged on that basis and not labeled as racists simply because of imagined prejudice, or even an offbeat racially tinged statement or act.

Observe that the charge of racism always goes in one direction. It is always a white person being racist towards some black victim. On the other hand, people make excuses when offenses are committed against a white person by a black individual, because the target of the offense is the "wrong" color. They tell us that it is impossible for black people to be racist towards white people, or that the offense or crime "was not racially motivated." We have examples of people making some of the most awful statements on a daily basis about white people, every single day in the media, and these statements are considered insightful, as edgy or "speaking truth to power."

There is a large segment of the population who are actually ok with the constant race baiting, and appeal to identity politics. They literally get angry at the people who highlight the damaging nature of this behavior. They are invested in the idea that America is a racist society toward black people, and they will stop at nothing to "prove" that this narrative is true. People who have lived exemplary lives can have all of the goodwill they have accumulated over their lifetime disappear for the slightest word slip, inappropriate comment, or moment of frustration.

Now, for the umpteenth time, no one is saying that racism does not exist. Of course it does. It would be foolish to think that in a country of almost 340 million people of so many different races, ethnic groups, religions and various other backgrounds that racism does not exist. But in the big picture, race is not the big issue that people make it out to be.

It is a political football that that has been weaponized to advance an agenda. Of course there are people who have had really terrible experiences that can be attributed directly to racism. In those instances society has to be honest, acknowledge the issue at hand, confront it aggressively, and put systems in place to make improvements, then keep moving forward.

Someone needs to explain why it is that when it comes to the issue of racism, so many Americans expect perfection. They absolutely refuse to treat it like they treat the other problems that exist in a society of imperfect people. They jump for joy whenever something happens that they can attribute to racism. That way they can triumphantly say "See I told you so." They then go on to gleefully paint "the system," and a whole group of people as racists because of an action that they either interpret to be racist or from time to time may really be a legitimate case of racism.

In this environment, it seems that people believe that the only reason anything bad ever happens to black people is because of racism. It does not matter how much the evidence in the everyday lives of black people contradict the narrative that black people are under siege, those invested in the idea that it is true will never accept it. They run to provide isolated incidents and other anecdotal "evidence" that "supports" their case. These people do not care that their constant appeal to race drives a wedge between Americans. They just want to promote the narrative.

In the case of white liberals, they get to present themselves as honest. They expect points, a pat on the back, and they expect to win favor from black people for "acknowledging their white privilege," and "speaking truth to power." In the meantime, spurred on by their white liberal Democrat enablers, too many black people latch on to the victim mentality. It is time to expose this racket for what it is, and for people to stop being scared about speaking out against it. It does not matter if people call you insensitive, privileged, uncaring, a sell out, coon, uncle tom, house nigger or any of the names that the people who are invested in keeping the divide going may call you. More people need to speak out.

This is so sad.

White Guilt, Black Victims

White guilt and black victims, what a combination! A bunch of
white liberals who so feel the need to assuage the weight of
guilt on their shoulders for sins committed by white people
before them, they encourage all kinds of bad behavior by black
people, and make excuses for them in the process.

These white lefties hold black people to such a low standard in
the name of being "woke." They pat themselves on their
shoulders, completely oblivious to the damage that they are
doing in the black community because of their actions.

Many in the black community look at these white leftists and
feel validated in their victim status as black people. They can
point to the "caring" white person, and say that even white
people agree with them, and understand their plight.

The white leftist then gets to go home feeling righteous, and
complimenting himself, as many of the people who they claim
to be fighting for continue to wallow in their imagined
predicament, believing there is no way out because they are
victims of "the man."

Check out this ludicrous, stupid, asinine tweet from a few years
ago by one of the white leftist enablers who thinks that she is
"woke." Her name is Emily Lakdawalla. She describes herself
as a "planetary evangelist" (whatever that is) for The Planetary
Society. This is what she said, referring to the movie Black

Panther "So I carefully did not buy tickets for opening weekend because I did not want to be the white person <u>sucking Black joy</u> out of the theater. What's the appropriate date for me to by tickets? Is next weekend ok?"

Now folks, are these people serious with this nonsense? There are at least ten troubling underlying questions all intertwined in this drivel that she tweeted, but there is no need to go through them all. Nevertheless, they are all questions screaming for answers.

See if you can figure out all of the stupidity wrapped up in that tweet. Delve into the mind of a self righteous liberal and see how little it suggests they think of black people.

As noted this is from a few years back, but it has grown one hundred fold since then.

If this does not blow your mind...This is the level of crazy, the level of stupid, the level of quackery, the level of nuttiness that we are up against.

We cannot shrink from the challenge.

This is not to complain, but to stir some to action.

Chapter 2

Black Men Dying

Another Look At The George Floyd Incident

Revisiting the George Floyd incident during the trial of officer Derek Chauvin, it was necessary to again look at the circumstances that brought us to the trial.

After the entire George Floyd video finally came out, we got to see what really happened leading up to his death. What the video actually revealed was completely against the narrative that the corrupt media promoted for months on end. Their misrepresentation of the facts led to months of daily rioting, looting, violence, killing, and general mayhem that is still reverberating even now in several cities.

We saw an uptick in violent crime in major cities as the corrupt media and race pimps everywhere continued to vilify the police. By the time the video that showed what really happened came out, the situation was already too far gone and out of control. In true drive by fashion, after the media created the chaos with their false narrative, they simply moved on to shoot up more unsuspecting victims with their brand of Kalashnikov journalism.

Derek Chauvin the man we all witnessed callously kneel on the neck of George Floyd definitely needed to be held to account for his actions, but the full video reveals that race played no part in what he did.

George Floyd was strung out on drugs. He was hyper and belligerent. He refused to cooperate with the police for well over a half of an hour. The police showed much patience in dealing with him while he continually refused to cooperate with their instructions. At one point while he was being uncooperative with the police in the police vehicle, Floyd shouted I can't breathe, I can't breathe…in the police car. This is before he was placed on the ground by the officers.

One of the more startling reveals in the video is that Floyd at one time even asked the police to lay him on the ground. When they moved him to the ground, he continued refusing to cooperate, and that is when officer Chauvin put his knee on Floyd's neck. That is when things took a fatal turn.

We all saw the part of the video where Floyd was pleading for the officer to remove his knee from his neck. Chauvin refused to let up even a little.

Regardless of what anyone may think about George Floyd, it was heartbreaking to see the way he died, especially when you consider that many of the people standing around were pleading with the officer to remove his knee off of Floyd's neck. Chauvin's action, callous as it was, may have stemmed from the frustration of Floyd's uncooperativeness over the previous 45 minutes.

Chauvin's training and professionalism should have led him to respond more appropriately, especially because he was the senior officer on the scene. He let his frustrations get the better of him. He will definitely have to account for that, but the idea that this man was some raging lunatic, out of control white police officer who hated black people, and was acting out on that hatred with George Floyd is a lie. It is a lie that has cost the country a lot.

The people who stirred up the race hysteria pushing the lie should be ashamed, but we know they will not be. They never wanted to get to the heart of the issue. As the left has told us with their own mouths. They do not ever want a crisis to go to waste.

The left can shout mission accomplished on this one.

Facts do not matter, appeasing the mob is more important, and the mob said get whitey

Fight back against the left or we'll descend deep and deeper into the abyss of leftist degradation.

The Left and Democrats Pretend to Care about the Deaths of Black Men

About 70, 000 black Americans died violent deaths over the last ten years. That is approximately 7,000 each year (check the FBI crime statistics database for yourself). Of those tens of thousands, the left and the Democrat party is only concerned about the death of one black man, perhaps two or three. The one they care about most died on 25 May 2020. The one death of a black man that raised the ire of leftists everywhere is the death of George Floyd.

Don't believe for one minute that these scammers care a thing about George Floyd or black people. It is impossible for these charlatans to care a micro fraction less.

George Floyd was nothing more to them than a convenient instrument that they could use to further their destructive propaganda that keeps black people in mental chains, and divide the country. The one thing the left fears more than anything is a free thinking, independent black mind that does not just go along with the crowd.

They fear a black mind that thinks, evaluates, assesses and makes decisions based on data, and what is actually happening on the ground in real time, in situations like the George Floyd saga.

The evil left and the Democrat Party knows that once they can emotionally rile up enough black people, then facts do not matter. Even after we know all the facts about what happened in the George Floyd incident, these shysters continue to push his death as a racist killing. Nothing ever came out in the trial that showed race was even a pico factor.

Keith Ellison, the Minnesota Attorney General and former vice chair of the Democrat National Party said the following, "I wouldn't call it that because hate crimes are crimes where there's an explicit motive and of bias." He said "We don't have any evidence that Derek Chauvin factored in George Floyd's race as he did what he did." Ellison went on to add, "If we'd had a witness that told us that Derek Chauvin made a racial reference, we might have charged him with a hate crime. But I would have needed a witness to say that on the stand. We didn't have it. So we didn't do it." The Attorney General then said something very interesting, he added, "In our society, there is a social norm that killing certain kinds of people is more tolerable than other kinds of people. In order for us to stop and pay serious attention to this case and be outraged by it, it's not necessary that Derek Chauvin had a specific racial intent to harm George Floyd." Mind you, Ellison himself was part of the mob that helped to fan the racist hysteria flames.

That last statement from Ellison is true, however the fact is that because most people bought in to the hysteria that Chauvin was killed because he is black, it set off a wave of violence and protests across the country based on a false narrative that continues up to today.

Imagine how different it could have been if Ellison had come out right after the killing, been the voice of calm and assured citizens that the Attorney General's office was going to leave no stone unturned in the pursuit of justice. How might things have been different if he had let people know early on that there was no indication it was a hate crime? Instead Ellison helped to initiate a feeding frenzy and remained silent as the left gorged to their hearts' content.

Nothing is sacred to the left. Nothing! It is part of their written ideology to use misfortune to further their agenda. For the left, the death of George Floyd was nothing more than a useful implement.

George Floyd's situation was tragic. Your anatomy would have to be missing a heart to not be hurt or outraged by what we saw in the George Floyd video. However, it had nothing to do with race. It had to do with sloppy police work by a frustrated police officer who lost his cool with an uncooperative suspect who was strung out on drugs. It had to do with a police officer who allowed his frustrations to make him abandon his training and cast away his professionalism in a highly volatile situation.

It's tragic. It's sad. It should not have happened, but it's the truth. Watching people continue to use this man's death to spread race mania is wild.

Observing so many black Americans willingly get played by people who do not care a thing about them is maddening.

The Dreadful Death Of Ahmaud Arbery And The Question Of Race

One more, time the question is put out to anyone who knows the answer. Why is it that the murder of a black man only seems to matter to so many black Americans, and white liberals if the victim was killed by the police or a white person under dubious circumstances? What is the reason for this? The carnage of black men at the hands of other black men never seems to generate an equal outcry like we see when a black man is killed at the hands of a cop (especially a white cop) or white citizen?

We saw the same nonsense with the killing of a young man in Georgia by the name of Ahmaud Arbery. Arbery's name continues to be used as a rallying cry for many blacks, and white race hustlers in their propaganda effort to paint America as a racist nation.

Now rest assured, people have the right to demand justice for Ahmaud Arbery if he was indeed gunned down like an animal for no just cause. Even if all the unsavory reports that came out about him are true, and he does indeed have a shady history it is unfortunate that he lost his life in the manner that he did. That is a topic worthy of discussion.

What do you say to his family? There are no comforting words to offer to those who loved and cared about him. They will have to carry the grief of losing their son for the rest of their lives. It is a heartbreaking and inconsolable loss, but for crying out loud, is it at all possible to seek justice without continuing to add fuel to the fire by turning, and insisting that the whole incident was about nothing but race?

 Investigate what happened. Get to the bottom of it. Hold people accountable, including officials, for any wrong doing they may have committed. But for goodness sake, there was no need to trample all over this man's grave to further the victim narrative. That case like so many others was not about black people being persecuted. It was about the three men involved in the killing.

If in the end it does come out that this was about race (yes racism does still exist), then let's confront it, deal with it honestly and make sure that the perpetrators pay the full penalty. Let's make sure that they do not get to spread their hate any more in society, then keep on moving.

Again, at the risk of monotony, just to reiterate, no one is saying that there is no racism. It is impossible to get rid of racism in an imperfect world, but there was absolutely no need to use this unfortunate incident as a reason for large numbers of black people to turn attention on themselves, and wallow around in the mud of victimhood. The chances of any black man getting killed by some random white dude who hates black men jogging in white neighborhoods is really small.

It is difficult to understand why pushing the victim narrative is so important to so many black Americans who seem to relish the death of black men, just to keep pushing the ridiculous idea that black people are under siege in America? Stop using the unfortunate circumstances of these men's deaths to further this divisive foolishness.

People should demand that authorities seek the truth and pursue justice, but could we stop pretending that everything is about race? Can we do that just for once? It is possible for people to be jerks without them being racist jerks. How about this? If we must have the discussion about the killing of black men, or murder in general, can we at least have an honest discussion? Does it always have to be so one sided? Can we at least once talk about the fact that black men have to worry more about being killed by other black men more than by any other group?

When it comes to violent crime, each group suffers at the hands of those in their own group. Whites are mostly the victims of other whites. Hispanics are the victims of other Hispanics , etc., but black Americans kill and violently attack more of their own than any other group in America (check the FBI crime statistics database for yourself). The gap is very wide. Black men even kill more Asians that Asians kill their own. That is just the reality. It is a harsh reality, but reality nevertheless (check the FBI crime statistics database for yourself).

Addressing these truths do not mean that black Americans are prone to violence because of their race. It does not mean that blacks are defected or that there is anything intrinsically wrong with the race. Black people are no different than any other group. People are people, but acknowledging these real problems will help to put black America in a winning position when confronting them. The first step to resolving a problem is acknowledging that a problem exists.

Black Americans who continue to use these genuinely awful events as a reason to indulge in group self pity need to stop. Stop getting excited about these "opportunities" to keep crying poor us. Stop turning everything that happens to individual black citizens into an issue about the persecution of the group as a whole.

The Hunting Of Black People

Lebron James: "We're literally hunted
EVERYDAY/EVERYTIME we step foot outside the comfort
of our homes! Can't even go for a damn jog man! Like WTF
man, are you kidding me?!?!?!?!?!? No man fr ARE YOU
KIDDING ME!!!!! I'm sorry Ahmaud (Rest In Paradise) and
my prayers and blessings sent to the….. heavens above to your
family!!"

Lebron James is a man with a powerful voice and a large
microphone. He is a strong family man, successful businessman
and has so much going for him. He knows the benefit of putting
his head down, hard work, staying committed and keeping
himself clean. Quite frankly there is a lot to admire about
Lebron James. He has accomplished so much more at a young
age than most of us ever will in a lifetime.

Could you imagine if someone with a powerful voice like his
was to use that voice as a megaphone that encouraged young
black men to take more responsibility for their actions and their
lives?

What if he was to use that voice to call on more black men to
follow his example of dedication, hard work, and commitment
for their own lives?

What if Lebron was to assume the posture of a victor and not a
victim, and encourage other young black men to do the same?

Could you imagine if Lebron was to use his voice as a voice of reason in situations like these, calling for justice but simultaneously using his very powerful voice as a soothing, healing balm?

What if?

Police Brutality, And Crime In The Black Community

Almost 7,000 U.S. Marines were killed at the battle of Iwo Jima During World War Two. It was one of the fiercest battles that U.S. Marines and Sailors fought against the mighty imperial Japanese Army over a 35 day period. If you would like to get a descriptive idea about the horrors of war, read about the battle of Iwo Jima.

In the United States every year the number of black men killed in homicides is close to the equivalent number of men who died at the battle of Iwo Jima. Over 90 percent of these black men killed, die at the hands of other black men (check the FBI crime statistics database).

Whenever people point to the amount of violence amongst the black citizenry to show the hypocrisy of those who only seem to complain when a black person is killed by the police or a white person, those pushing the narrative of black oppression get offended.

They say that pointing out the obvious, that blacks are mostly killed by other blacks is a deflection. The deflection is a means of taking attention away from the blatant abuse of black people by others in the society. They then say people generally commit crimes in the communities where they live.

After that they scream, nobody talks about white on white crime. Nobody talks about Asian on Asian crime. Nobody talks about Hispanic on Hispanic crime. Nobody talks about Native American on Native American crime. "Why is it that every time people attempt to point out the obvious brutality of the police against black people, or the violence committed by white people against black people like we saw with George Floyd, and Ahmaud Arbery that everyone deflects to 'so called' black on black crime?"

Well, the answer to that is simple. True, people commit crime in the communities wherever they live. Here is the difference though. When it comes to crime in any community, whether it be white on white crime, Hispanic on Hispanic crime or any other group, no ethnic group/race slaughters or engages in violence against their own like black people do against their own. When it comes to crimes committed against other ethnic groups, no other group is as prolific as blacks. The numbers are staggering. Now that statement is either true or it is not. It does not matter how one feels about that information.

Is it a verifiable fact or is it a lie?

When it comes to unwarranted acts of violence by the police against black people, the numbers pale in comparison to the carnage that takes place in the black community. They are not even close. So pointing out the staggering number of blacks killed by other blacks is not to suggest that society should not be outraged when others point to the <u>rare cases of outright police abuse</u>. People should be outraged.

The police have been entrusted with a huge responsibility in caring for it's citizens. Balancing that care and protection, with the authorization of the state to use violence against its citizens is a very sensitive issue. When that trust is betrayed it causes a sense of helplessness and sometimes people feel a need to lash out. It's understandable.

These emotions however should never give way to the realities that are actually happening on the ground. The truth is that over the last fifty years the killing of black citizens by the police has declined significantly to the point where it rarely happens.

Yes, this goes against the narrative and the propaganda put out by the Democrat Party and the media, but it is the truth. Now, acknowledging this does not mean that we should not strive to do even better. We should not be callous to the death of anyone, but the responsibility to do better lies with everyone, not just the police.

The police are often called to operate in a dark seedy world where the worst of human nature is often on display. In that world, violence and intimidation are common tools that are used to fulfill some of the most animalistic desires. The acts of brutality, the disregard for human life, and the depths of depravity that people go to in the criminal world in pursuit of their unholy goals are unimaginable. The live in a degenerate world into which few enter voluntarily, and where bottom feeders thrive.

It so happens that a large number of the people who operate in this world are black. It is a natural consequence that the police would have more encounters and interactions with black people as a result of this reality, and because of it; there is more opportunity for things to go wrong between the police and black citizens.

We can honestly address the issue of police brutality when it does occur. In fact as a society we are duty bound to do it. It does not matter that it happens rarely. Let us address it whenever it happens but we also have to address the issue of criminal behavior by a section of black citizens who gives the whole community a bad name.

So, it's not that police brutality does not matter. The point is that there is a much bigger problem that needs attention. It is the rhinoceros in the room. Let's address it.

How Should We Deal With The Shooting Death Of A Black Man By The Police?

Every life lost at the hands of the police will be mourned by those who loved the victim, regardless of the circumstances under which they lost their lives. When an innocent person is killed at the hands of the police as apparently happened in Oklahoma a few years ago when a white female officer killed a black man, it is particularly heart wrenching for those close to, and who knew the person killed.

One cannot imagine the heart ache that a mother feels when she gets the news that her son has been killed, wives will be inconsolable, children will sob their hearts out when they learn that daddy will never be coming home again. Friends and other family members will be in a state of shock as they ask the eternal question. Why?

It will be heartless to dismiss the raw emotions that people feel in the aftermath of these circumstances. No one with a conscience or a heart can be so cruel to discard what these people go through in their moments of grief. It is no comfort to tell a grieving relative that this type of stuff only happens once in a while; that it is not as big a deal as people make it out to be. Stuff happens! These words mean nothing to those suffering the sudden, unexpected loss of a loved one.

As a people (Americans), we must empathize with those who find themselves in these unfortunate circumstances.

Investigators must leave no stone unturned in getting to the bottom of the issue. Authorities must ensure that justice is dispensed.

Despite the need to empathize with the unfortunate and the grieving, it is important to not let the whole discussion get hijacked by those whose only interest is to stir racial discord amongst the people. The unfortunate loss of a young black man's life at the hands of the police under unfortunate and tragic circumstances presents another opportunity for members of the victocracy to rage against the imaginary epidemic of police killing innocent black men.

The race hustlers come out in full force every time, preying on the unwarranted fears of many in the black community. Cases go from being isolated instances that need to be addressed, to discussions about the targeting of black men in America. We must not allow the Eric Dysons, the Marc Lamont Hills, the Jesse Jacksons, Al Sharptons, and Ibram X Kendis of the world to be the preeminent voices that manage to shut out all others.

Because of incidents like these, many black people only look outward, expending a lot of emotional energy. They channel a lot of rage in the wrong direction for the problems that ail a significant segment of black America. The voice of reason must be there to challenge the promulgators of dissension who often spew a lot of bile in times of tragedy, distrust and uncertainty.

Many of these swindlers spend their time looking for reasons to be offended. They relish the spotlight and the opportunity to spread their message of deception. The real problems facing many in the black community that need to be addressed will continue to be neglected and ignored.

As the victim class continues to express outrage, dissatisfaction, and their disgust at the system, the race pimps snicker to themselves. They are incredulous every time they manage to pull the wool over the eyes of the victim posse. The pimps laugh all the way to the bank.

Many black people, blissfully unaware of being duped will continue pushing the narrative that black men are under siege. Perspective will mean nothing to the mob. The application of critical thinking will not even be an afterthought. Emotions above all else is what will rule. Evidence, be damned! There is none so blind as those who will not see.

In the case of the Oklahoma shooting, it looked like the police clearly shot the man while he was not a threat to their lives in any way. That was the issue. That was the situation that needed to be addressed. There was no need to inject race into the equation just because the victim was black and the officer white.

It is terrible enough that the man lost his life. There was absolutely no need to exacerbate the situation and turn it into another false crusade against police brutality.

In the end the police officer was tried in a court of law with a mixed jury that consisted of men, women, black and white jurors. They listened to the evidence and rendered their verdict. The prosecution did not prove their case. It is not always as the race brothel runners make it out to be.

To repeat a broken record, in a country of three hundred plus million people, with the police having tens of thousands of interactions every day with the public, there is a very high probability that something will go wrong.

Police work by nature is dangerous, and it is highly stressful. The police are human. They get scared. They are often on edge. Sometimes they make mistakes and other times they do the wrong thing. These people interact with the dregs of society on a level that most of us will never experience in our lifetime.

Let's identify problems together when they do occur. Let's fight to make the corrections that bring about change. When incidents happen, deal with the situations at hand. Do not allow them to degenerate into campaigns against the police.

The Inconvenient Truth About Crime, The Police, And Black Men

When will the media begin addressing the difficult truths that a certain section of black America needs to hear?

Here it is folks!

Police go where crime is. Crime is the problem in too many areas where black people live!

Police have no choice but to go where crime is committed. It so happens that a very big amount of violent crime takes place in black neighborhoods across the country. The problem is crime in too many areas where black people live. The police are not the problem. Crime is the problem. Where crime is, the likelihood of things going wrong increases exponentially.

This failure to take responsibility for actions is going to get more and more black people killed, then each time something tragic happens the police will get blamed, and that will trigger a race riot.

As long as the media, politicians, celebrities, academia and other dishonest people continue to tell black people that they bear no responsibility for any of the tragic outcomes in their interactions with the police, then the problem of police shooting black men will not go away.

Stop being confrontational with the police. Don't continue to needlessly escalating these police encounters. Cooperate with the police. Be respectful and take up any legitimate complaint that you have with the police after your encounter with them. Stop this nonsense of being disrespectful, confrontational, non cooperative and aggressive toward the police.

It is likely to go wrong with more black men coming out on the wrong side of the bargain.

If as a society we do not wake up and acknowledge what is the very real problem of violent crime in many areas where black people live, then nothing will change.

All over the TV there are white liberals and rich, privileged, black people telling black America that they are victims of the police and the white man's system. They say that black men are getting killed for no other reason than being black. They talk about black people getting killed for wearing a hoodie and a lot of other nonsense.

They repeat all of these lies over and over and over without ever giving the actual numbers. Absent from all of the rhetoric about the so called carnage of black people at the hands of the police is the raw, hard data.

They just play on the emotions of black people when a black person is killed under tragic circumstances. They use it to continue the lie that black people are being mowed down in the streets.

It is a lie!

The police go where crime is, and crime is rampant in many black neighborhoods where a handful of black people terrorize their communities.

These white liberals who are constantly selling the black victim narrative to black people are not the friends of black people. They are only signaling their virtue at the expense of black men who are needlessly getting killed.

White liberals who make themselves feel good by telling black people that it is racism and not crime, or their behavior towards the cops that are getting black people killed, are dangerous people.

Stop it!

Chapter 3

The Black Leadership Mafia

Charlatan Leaders in the Black Community

The killing of Michael Brown in 2015, and the rioting that followed was symptomatic of larger problems that people face in so many of America's inner cities. The events had a familiar ring to it, but the answer to the problems required the application of a different remedy. In order to find possible solutions though, it was imperative to honestly address the root causes of the endless turmoil that takes place in so many cities around America.

When incidents like what happened with Brown occur, much of the anger that we saw on display, and directed against the police in particular was the direct result of black people being fed the narrative that every negative occurrence in their lives is because of the white man who hates them, and wants to systematically subjugate them. This lie has been fed to black people through constant repetition by one political party over decades. Many black people have believed the lie. What we observe today in America every time a black man is killed under horrible circumstances, are the fruits of the discontent that have led to the perception created by the lie.

The shameful, irresponsible act of perpetually stirring discontent in black communities has been used by one political party in order to secure the black vote. Black people in return faithfully continue to reward those politicians who champion themselves as their saviors. These politicians will then rescue black people from whatever ails them, and the supposed injustices they face daily.

The insidious strategy has worked so well that many black people now find themselves in a situation where they believe that they must continue to elect these politicians who promise them the world. These self-appointed saviors never deliver on their promises, but they give black people enough handouts to keep them coming back for more. What they give is never enough to elevate the black communities they serve out of their desperate circumstances. Black people as a result become stuck in the same situation decade after decade, never making it past the revolving door of their existence.

Many black people stubbornly refuse to try something different. They elect the same people from the same political party, getting the same results over, and over, and over again. Under the leadership of these people, many blacks have experienced nothing but misery. They see this as an act of self-preservation because they have been led to believe that everyone else has sinister intentions toward them. They believe that in trying something different their situation will be much worse.

Anyone who takes a dispassionate look at the data, and carefully examines it will see a common thread that runs through it. The poorest cities across America that have been plagued by the problems of high crime, failing schools, chronic unemployment or underemployment, public corruption and other social problems, have almost exclusively been run by leftist politicians. These politicians who pander to the people, are beholden to teachers unions, other special interests and implement economic policies that do not work.

They attribute all of these problems not to their policies, but to nebulous outside forces. They blame the rich for the problems of the poor. They hardly ever take the side of law and order. They constantly malign the police. They portray white people as villains. They blame their failing schools on lack of funding. They make promises they cannot keep, and they never look inwardly to solve any of their problems. In the process, the problems in these cities become worse, negatively affecting the people they claim to represent. In all of this, blacks and other minorities are the ones mostly affected, suffering the consequences of all these actions.

The party that governs these cities has pulled off one of the simplest yet most ingenious schemes in political history. It is the equivalent of wolves watching the sheep barn. Many black people find themselves trapped in a vicious cycle of under privilege in the cities run by leftist Democrats who have free rein to implement the policies they see fit. When their policies fail, they then claim that "the system" is at fault though they run the system.

Black people in these communities meanwhile continue to buy in to the conspiracy and blame others for all of their problems. They then vote the same people back into power, and the pattern continues. In this environment, black people can always blame others for their own problems. They get to avoid taking responsibility for their actions, (including their voting) and their lives. They can then continue to "justifiably" direct their anger at the rich, white people, the police and anyone they have been told is the cause of their problems. They see no contradiction in attacking and opposing the police in their crime ridden neighborhoods, burning down businesses, and attacking innocent people. In their minds, nothing is ever their own fault. It is the system that is to blame.

To be clear, no political party has any magical formula to get rid of the problems in the areas plagued by these issues, and the many challenges that they face. No policy, no matter how effective in theory will work if people are not willing to make the hard choices, and the sacrifices that are sometimes necessary to bring about change. In addition, if people are not willing to play a more active role in their own lives, and take responsibility for their actions, things will remain the same.

Black people should seriously reconsider their political alliance.

Those who truly want to see black people elevate themselves should work harder to reach black communities in helping them to see that there is indeed a better way. Their fellow Americans want them to succeed. Help them acknowledge where they need to make changes in their own lives.

Gaslighting On Racial Discord

When it comes to gas lighting on race, no one does it like the
Obamas.

Michelle Obama and her husband Barrack Hussein Obama the
great engage in some of the most shameless race shoveling that
is even imaginable. These people continue to stoke fear among
black citizens, constantly telling them that life in the United
States is a hellish, dystopian cesspool. It is just shameless what
they do. It is revulsive.

The question is, why would these people continue to do this.
Why would these successful people with such inspiring stories
continue to tell black people that the world is against them?
Why would they insist America hates black people? Why would
they preach the message to blacks that for blacks to get ahead
blacks must remember that they are starting 20 paces behind?
What is that all about?

What is the motivation behind this dark message they keep
promulgating to black people?

Yes, there is racism that exists because we live in an imperfect
world. People do terrible things to each other. That is just the
world that we live in, but the idea that black people cannot get
ahead because of racism is just nonsense. Why are they
constantly stoking this unreasonable fear among black people?
How is this helpful?

Black people in this country need to wake up and stop buying into this foolishness. Blacks are being played by people with an evil agenda meant to keep blacks in the bondage of fear. Perched from their million dollar mansion, with their multi-million dollar Netflix contract, with their children attending the finest schools, their high level security, and all of their privileges; Michelle Obama, Barrack Obama, and their Democrat political allies continue to tell black people that in America blacks cannot expect positive things to happen to the black population. The system is designed to keep black people down for no other reason than that they are black.

This is wrong what they are doing and it's getting people killed.

Black America, hear the other side of the story. Dare to look elsewhere for more perspective.

Michelle the Bella O' And The Black Vote (Written in response to Michelle O's diatribe May 2020)

Hey black people! Yeah, all you with the extra melanin. Michelle Obama is mad at you. She expressed her frustration over you in her soon to be released documentary. Why was Michelle O' mad at all of you with your dark skin hue? Well, ya didn't show up and vote Democrat in the 2016 Presidential Elections. Because of you black people, because of you Hillary Clinton is not President of the United States, carrying on the legacy of Barrack Hussein O' the magnificent (give praise to his name for he is great).

You did not get the memo, black US citizens? You'd better get yourself in line and get with the program. What's that…earn your vote? Who do you think you are black man? Who do you think you are black woman? You need to stop acting as though you have a mind of your own…talking about earn your vote. Democrats don't have to work for your vote. You are black! They don't have to earn your vote at all. All they have to do is call the other guy or the other gal a racist, and then you go do your duty black dude. Do your duty black chick.

You just get on down to the voting booth and give your vote to whoever the Democrat running for office is. You heard Michelle! Well, just in case you didn't get it, Michelle went on to elaborate. "The people who didn't vote at all, the young people, the women, that's when you think, man, people think this is a game," she continued. "It wasn't just in this election.

Every midterm. Every time Barack didn't get the Congress he needed, that was because our folks didn't show up. After all that work, they just couldn't be bothered to vote at all. That's my trauma."

Hope you were paying attention to Michelle talk about "our folks." That's right! You have already been told, you don't have your own mind. You don't get to think and make decisions for yourself. You are their folks, and as their folks; you just go ahead and vote Democrat. Forget that the woman she wanted you to vote for is the grand champion of flooding black neighborhoods with abortion clinics that have helped to keep the black population stagnated for decades, as twenty million black babies have been denied seeing the light of day since Roe vs Wade.

Yeah black people, do as Michell says and vote for the people who fight for the rights of illegal immigrants over the rights of United States citizens. Vote for the people who stand on the sidelines cheering and promoting the growth of the illegal population from all across Latin America, as the black population simultaneously, and artificially remains static as a result. Who cares!?! Just go ahead and vote for the people who tell you that your daughters have to share locker rooms, and bathrooms with boys who call themselves girls. Put your support behind the people who enthusiastically, and aggressively defend the rights of boys who call themselves girls to compete against your daughters in sports. Vote for the people who would bring the weight of government against you, and force you to bake a cake for a gay wedding against the deep convictions of your own conscience.

Vote for the people who have been running black inner cities where crime is rampant, poverty is widespread, and education is substandard. Just ignore the fact that the people who send their own children to private schools would deny you the right to do the same. This is done by them consistently coming out against school vouchers that have been key in raising the standard of education for some black children.

No, none of that matters. Pay no attention to their constant race baiting, their insistence on portraying you as victims, or their awful policies. What matters most of all is that you are black. They don't have to compete for your vote. It is your duty to them, even if they can't tell you exactly why, and besides, orange man baahhhd. So there!

Michelle O, Demagogue Extraordinaire

Michelle Obama in one of her past interviews stated that people are now dismissive of the Presidency because her husband, a black man, was not too long ago the President of the United States. She went on to add, "I guess it's kind of like if the black guy can do it, anybody can do it and that's not true. It's a hard job."

So according to Michelle, everyday Americans in over 500 counties around the country who voted twice for her amazing hubby, have reverted back to their racist ways. After the reign of Barrack the Great, they said "oh that was easy…shoots, and a black dude did it with such ease too…ah the Presidency must not be all it's cracked up to be."

This is what they think of you.

Again, just to reiterate, this woman who told us that until her husband, the anointed one, Barrack Hussein Obama (praise be unto his name) was nominated to run for President, she had no reason to be proud of her country, is now telling the rest of the nation that because a black man was not too long ago the President, people now dismiss the Presidency. These people…

What do you say to that? How does a woman like this develop such disdain for her country? How does she formulate such a low opinion of her fellow citizens? For people like Michelle Obama, no matter how far they go in life, no matter how much they achieve, no matter the opportunities they've been afforded, they can never rid themselves of the racist bogeyman. For them, lurking around every corner is a white man whose sole purpose in life is to destroy them. Every shadow is a racist gun just waiting to open fire on them.

There is nothing that anyone can do that will ever convince them that generally speaking, people are not trying to do them harm. They believe that as long as this world remains imperfect, and as long as bad things sometimes happen, there is no reason to be appreciative of all the good things that exist in their life.

Michelle Obama who at the time she was voicing this opinion, polls were telling us is the most admired woman in the world, is a world class demagogue. She is a flame thrower, a gas lighter who continues to add fuel to all the racial discord that exists in this country. It is because so many listen and give credence to people like her that too many black people continue to see themselves as second class citizens in America.

They refuse to live as free men and women because they believe what Michelle and her ilk say. They will have a cow over Donald Trump telling people that if they hate the country so much they can go back to their country of origin, fix it then come back and show us how it is done. These same people will have absolutely no problem with race hustlers like Michelle Obama making these awful statements. It is not that she said this about a few people who she believes think this way, but about tens and tens of millions of Americans.

Oh, she's dignified alright. She has an air of sophistication that Donald Trump will never be able to match, but she is more dangerous precisely for this reason. She has credibility. So when she says that people dismiss the Presidency now because a black guy was recently President, instead of pushing back on such a divisive statement, people shake their heads approvingly. It's a fact in their minds. After all if such a thoughtful, intelligent woman like Michelle O is saying it, there must be something to it, right?

When the people who support Donald Trump heard demagogues like this woman talk, and they hear people defend statements like what she made, and make excuses for her, their support for Trump increased. Whereas with Trump, a lot of mind reading and interpretation of words is required to come up with one's opinion of him, people like Michelle Obama tell the country over and over who they are and what they think.

These are really sick people who hide behind a veneer of sophistication to spread their animus. People can support them if they wish, while ignoring the substance of what they say, believe and do. But please save the lectures, the fake selective outrage and the posturing for another day. No one on the other side wants to hear it.

Michelle And Barrack, Victims Of America's Hate

Michelle Obama launched her book tour a while back. In an interview with Robin Roberts, Michelle, the race instigator, stated that "Our presence had been celebrated by millions of Americans, but it also contributed to a reactionary sense of fear and resentment among others."

She went on to state that "The hatred was old and deep and as dangerous as ever." She did not give any specific examples of the hatred, or the so called reactionary sense of fear and resentment she was talking about, but that is not necessary in her world. Being the victim is a cherished status, and worth holding onto with every fiber of ones being. It does not matter how successful, accomplished, intelligent, influential or admired a person may be. Make no mistake; Michelle Obama is all of those things.

Despite all of that though, Michelle has to hold on to the notion that she is reviled by a large section of Americans. They hate her for no other reason than the color of her skin. This woman who has been in the company of royals, and treated like royalty herself wants us to know that despite her privilege, she is after all just a black woman in America. Michelle wants anyone who would listen to know that her pigmentation more than anything matters to a large segment of Americans who rabidly hate her for it.

Of course the sycophantic media, in the pursuit of promoting leftist ideology has completely abandoned its role. The press simply allows this race enticing madame to make all of these statements unchallenged. She is never asked to give details pertaining to the claims she makes about race.

These media personalities, like a bunch of groupies, are in awe of her, and just content to be in her presence. Journalistic integrity be damned! Asking probing questions is reserved for those of the conservative persuasion.

No one who has followed Mrs. Obama's career is surprised by her assertion that her fellow citizens were fearful and resentful of her and her husband's presence in the White house. Remember this is the woman who said that she only became proud of her country for the first time in her entire lifetime, when her husband was chosen as the Democrat Party representative to run for President in 2008. Prior to that Mrs. Obama had no reason whatsoever to be proud of her country.

Do not forget also that she and her husband for twenty years sat in a church that preached on black liberation theology. They sat at the feet of a man who vehemently hates America, and has often spewed racist rhetoric towards white people from his pulpit. It's not the kind of rhetoric that requires interpretation. It's naked, unadulterated, hateful rhetoric.

Many black people reading Mrs. Obama's contention that because of her color, her family's presence caused Americans to be fearful and resentful will shake their head in agreement. They will not require that she back up her statement with any proof. Just the fact that the Obamas are black is enough reason to conclude that any opposition to them was based on race.

It is sickening. It is disgusting, but it will continue to pass as insightful, nuanced, sophisticated and deep.

The people who will lap this stuff up without an ounce of curiosity are the same people who dare to lecture the rest of the country about their support for Donald Trump. They see nothing wrong in this woman arbitrarily, without anything at all to back up her claims, accusing her fellow Americans of being resentful towards her family because her family is black. That is not divisive to them. She is just "telling it like it is."

How does one reconcile Mrs. Obama's statement with the treatment that they had received for eight long years? They were practically worshipped during their entire tenure, but that does not matter. The fact that they faced opposition at all rendered them as victims of hate and resentment. Criticizing them was anathema, and anyone who dared to break that sacred rule felt the wrath of their defenders.

Looking back on the Obama years, one could only wander what would have been possible had they taken a different approach, and been cheerleaders for the country, talking of all that is possible for anyone blessed enough to be born here. Instead, what we had for eight years was a man beloved by so many, telling the country over and over, and over again how terrible and racist it is.

His wife continues to spread the message that in America your effort and achievements do not matter. Just the color of your skin matters.

Colin Kaepernick, Lebron James, Spike Lee, Oprah Winfrey and the whole cabal of race gladiators are in good company.

Barrack Obama Race Baiter Supreme At His Absolute Worst

Barrack Obama showed up at the <u>funeral of John Lewis</u> and held a political rally. OOOOHHH, Mr. man himself was in full flight. He called for the elimination of the filibuster. He called it a relic of the Jim Crow past. Anyone who knows how the filibuster works understands that it is a check on unfettered power by any one political party. Even in a Democracy, power can corrupt, and the filibuster was created so that no one party would be able to pass any kind of law without push back. Mr. hope and change called it a relic of the Jim Crow past.

He said that Bull Connor is gone (don't ever forget by the way that, Bull Connor was a Democrat), but today we witness police kneeling on the necks of black Americans. Kneeling on the necks of black Americans, really? This guy…no Mr. Obama! We saw a bad policeman kneel on the neck of a U.S. citizen in an incident of bad police work that no one thinks was right. The citizen happened to be black. This is not standard operating procedure for the police, and Obama knows this. What the policeman did was wrong, but it does not automatically make him a racist. Barrack Obama knows this, but there is no political leverage to gain by acknowledging this. This guy…

Obama continued, "George Wallace (another Democrat) may be gone, but the Federal Government is using tear gas and batons against peaceful demonstrators." Here we had Obama comparing federal agents doing their job enforcing the law against violent mobs, to George Wallace. People trying to burn down federal buildings, leaving a trail of blood, mayhem and destruction are portrayed as innocent protesters, while the law enforcement officers are vilified. This guy...

The crowd that was there to celebrate the life of John Lewis while simultaneously mourning his passing applauded. No one found this kind of talk to be repugnant at a funeral in 2020 America. As long as the liberal agenda is advanced, that is all that matters.

Obama claimed that political opponents are targeting minorities with restrictive voter ID laws and "attacking our voting laws with surgical precision," at the time...in 2020 America. And the crowd stood up to applaud the messiah as he talked about the United States in 2020 like it's 1956. This guy...

The truth is that Barrack Obama and his lefty allies infantilize black people by talking about them like they are helpless children. They do this to continue pushing the victim narrative. Obama and his band of demonizers talk about ID card laws like these laws are crippling obstacles for black people.

Elections are held every two years. In the case of Presidential elections, they are held every four years. Barrack Obama and the Democrat Party junta want all Americans to know that between these two year and four year timelines, black people are so stupid, so incapable of doing for themselves, so under served and down on their luck, that they cannot get themselves ID cards. This guy…

He peddled mail in ballots and every other leftist dream at the funeral service. This man of privilege who rode that wave of privilege, opportunity and euphoria, from all the way across the Pacific in the exotic land of Indonesia, to his private school on the scenic shores of Hawaii, to Occidental College, to the Harvard law review board, to the Senate, all the way to the White House, to his multimillion dollar mansion; he continues to tell everyone else that while life was dandy for him, it is hell for everyone else, especially "the blacks." This guy…

But who is really surprised by Obama? This is the same guy who showed up at the funeral of five slain police officers a few years ago, and right there during the funeral; he accused the police of waging all out war on black men. He did this at the funeral of police officers killed by a black man who felt that he had the right to execute police officers. The shooter believed that the police wantonly kill black men. That is the Obama we are talking about after all.

Tell you what folks! Jesus Christ said that no one is good, because we all are imbued with the sinful nature…but this guy…this fellow called Barrack Obama… For all the talk about Trump, this Obama guy is the worst kind of awful.

No one willingly opens up their homes to vipers, cobras, or any other kind of snake. However, dress a snake up in a suit and teach that snake to act in a dignified manner, and those doors swing wide open. But that snake is still a snake! By the time people realize it, it's too late.

This is a dangerous, dangerous man.

Trump ain't got nothing on this dude!

Chapter 4

Post Slavery Black Liberation

A Message to All Independent Black Men

To all the independent thinking black men who have a contrary message of hope, keep your head up. Continue preaching your message of optimism. You have reason to be optimistic. Your expectation of positive things is based on a firm grip on reality. In the face of all the America hating, do not stop telling young black men that they have no reason to despair. They are enormously blessed to live in this country where they have tremendous opportunities to achieve their goals and be successful.

Instill in them a healthy respect for honest work, and for hard work. Remind them that even if it is true that they will face an element of prejudice in their lives that is unique to them, they can still rest assured that most Americans of every color and ethnic background want them to be successful. Remind them that the mechanisms to help them succeed are firmly in place, and within their grasp.

Let them know that they do not have to walk around encumbered with the notion that the system is designed to keep them down. Help those who believe the lie to cast off the chains of mental slavery that keep so many young black men from reaching their full potential.

Warn them against assuming the posture of a victim lest they begin to act like victims. Encourage them to reject the cynicism that leads to a life of self-pity and truly serves to keep them down. Convey to them that knowledge, and a mind that is willing to learn a different way are keys to help them unleash their latent ability. This will enable them to live a life exploding with possibility.

Teach them to laugh at the mockers who will call them Uncle Tom for adopting this attitude, and embracing this positive outlook on life. Let them know that a blessed life is not one that is free of trials (unpleasant things sometimes happen). Help them to see that obstacles and difficulties can be used as ingredients that lead to growth and blossoms into a truly fruitful life.

Last of all remind them that God is on their side. Tell them that by God's grace and mercy, through his son Jesus Christ, and his everlasting love they can do all things through his strength.

Black and Free

To all the autonomous, liberated black people out there. Continue on about your business like you always do, unencumbered by the paranoid mentality that there is some nebulous system out there actively trying to do you harm. Walk freely while others choose to continue wearing the shackles ordered for them by the plantation owners who wish to keep them enslaved to the narrative that they are under siege, and that their only refuge is to remain a slave of the plantation. You risk being called a coon ass nigga, an Uncle Tom or a sell out because you refuse to walk around angry at the so called system. However, you know who you are.

You are no one's slaves! You will not be forced to conform to a herd like mentality that requires no intellectual scrutiny or curiosity from you. You understand that the propaganda machine can only survive if it is not resisted. Do not become a captive to it. Hold your head up high with your shoulders squared as you keep moving forward. Be fearless in the face of obstacles. Even when it is tempting to do so, do not give in to the sheep mindset that forces you to start feeling sorry for yourself. Remember that no one ever walks through life problem free.

The problems that you face are not an indication that everything is terrible in America or in the world. You understand well that a country free of racism, and other ills is a Utopian dream that exists nowhere in this present world. Do not let the difficulties that you will surely face define who you are. Remember that how you handle adversity helps to determine your character. Your numbers are few. There is much to overcome. Keep in mind that together you can accomplish anything by helping to change the narrative. Be strong, be of good courage and remember that God is on your side.

The Safety of the Plantation

To the many black people who do not, it is time to dare think outside of the box that politicians for generations have told black people is their domain. The plantation on which so many people have attempted to keep black people on is one filled with goodies. These people say stay there where it's safe. We will take care of you. You will not have to worry about anything.

They demonize those who offer many black people the chance to be free. With freedom, and the opportunity to determine ones own destiny comes danger that you will never face on the plantation, because after all; the plantation is safe. If you are sick, the master will take care of you. If you need food, the master will feed you. The master will give you a place to lay your head, and will use all of these goodies to keep you where you are while he remains in power.

The master tells you that those who offer you freedom do not have your long-term interest at heart. With freedom comes the chance of failure. Freedom is risky, it is uncertain. With the opportunity to be free also comes the opportunity to realize your fullest potential, something that you will never get the chance to do on the plantation where it is safe. You will never be in control on the plantation.

These are the words of Frederick Douglass, the celebrated abolitionist, former slave, and statesman extraordinaire: "What shall we do with the Negro?" I have had but one answer from the beginning. Do nothing with us! Your doing with us has already played the mischief with us. Do nothing with us! If the apples will not remain on the tree of their own strength, if they are worm eaten at the core, if they are early ripe and disposed to fall, let them fall! I am not for tying or fastening them on the tree in any way, except by nature's plan, and if they will not stay there, let them fall. And if the Negro cannot stand on his own legs, let him fall also. All I ask is, give him a chance to stand on his own legs! Let him alone!

BLEXIT!

What is Blexit really? It stands for black exit.

Blexit is a movement sweeping the nation that dares black people to exit the bondage of the left and the Democrat Party. Blexit challenges black people to make a return to the traditional values that were the glue that held many black families together. The values of these people gave black people the strength to survive the arduous journey of their unique American story.

Don't forget values like faith in God, love of family, ambition and drive. Blexit tells black people that they do not have to awake each day with a mindset they are starting from a disadvantage. Blexit encourages black people to see themselves as full fledged Americans with as much of a chance at being successful as any other group in America, even though they may face some unique circumstances.

Blexit tells black people to confront their struggles, and just keep on moving. They do not need to stand still, feeling sorry for themselves. They do not have to blame the ubiquitous evil system. Blexit encourages the victor mentality in black people, not the victim mentality.

Black Americans are not stupid. They are not any less capable of making smart decisions and pursuing the opportunities that will give them the best opportunity to succeed. The reality though is that many black people have been fed so much poison over a long period of time, they respond more favorably to emotional stimuli than to facts on the ground. The issue is not that they cannot think, but that they will not think when it comes to certain issues.

Blexit encourages them to use their minds as the antidote to the poison that too many black people have been fed by the Democrat Party over the years. Blexit encourages them to begin to experiencing a cleansing of the mind that allows them to be mentally free.

One of the things that Democrats and the left has been most successful in achieving in America is the secularization of the culture by casting God into the garbage can. Blexit encourages black people to return to God and the values that were once pillars among the black citizenry.

Despite the popularity of Blexit though, the movement is never featured in the mainstream media. Don't expect to see a feature on any of the great personalities prominent in the Blexit movement any time soon on any of the major networks, except of course Fox News. The media is beholden to the Democrat Party and has a vested interest in promoting the status quo. The media fears strong, black independent thinkers. The media understands that these black people are a threat to the left. Therefore, the media will do anything and everything in its power to keep black people in the same spot.

A Message to Black Lives Matter: Let's Work On Us

To the Black Lives Matter movement, in the interest of really working to improve the plight and the lives of black people in this country, please take your message into the black neighborhoods where crime is rampant. Confront the perpetrators who inflict the most violence against other black people. Address the chronic issue of black on black crime and the sheer brutality with which it is often committed.

Because black lives are valuable, place more focus on the value of the black lives lost as a direct result of the wanton violence inflicted by other blacks on these victims. Work on decreasing the number of homicide victims in these communities where the murder rate is so significantly higher than in any other ethnic group. Because black lives matter, challenge the drug pushers in black communities to channel their energy into outreach programs that stress the importance of education, and work toward reducing the high school dropout rate. Because black lives matter so much, target more energy on the issue of absent black fathers from the home, and their children's lives. Perhaps reducing the rate of black children born to single parents from 73 percent may contribute significantly in addressing that issue.

Because black lives matter so much we should teach our young men the proper way to respond to and deal with the police when they are stopped by them (whether they are justifiably stopped or not). If we want to decrease the rate of incarceration amongst black men, we have to do a better job of getting them to understand that prison is a natural consequence of committing crime. Remind them that despite the rhetoric, there is no conspiracy by the Police against them. Tell them that the system, contrary to popular opinion, is not out to get them.

Teach young black men to carry themselves with pride and not assume the status of victims, encourage them to adopt a positive lifestyle with good habits and life changing behavior. Let them know that the American Dream is possible even for them.

If the Black Lives Matter movement, together with the rest of the community work diligently to help implement these simple measures in the black community, we will go a long way toward improving the lives of black people throughout this country.

Black Political Liberation, The Time Has Come

If you are a black person living in America today, and your biggest fear is the Klu Klux Klan or white supremacy, there's no other way to put this than to lovingly tell you that you are living in a mental prison. This is a prison of your own making with lots of assistance from the left, the media and the Democrat Party.

This call is an invitation to free yourself from those self-binding chains. Move into the realm of the liberated. Scream it from the rooftops that you are a victor, not a victim. Stop walking around with the mindset that in America you are a second class citizen. You are not!

See yourselves as full fledged Americans with the same rights, privileges, and range of boundless opportunities to succeed right at your fingertips. These opportunities exist for any other individual or group in this country.

Reject the naysayers who constantly tell you that the only way for you to make it in America is to have the back of one hand in the palm of the other, with sad puppy eyes, barely looking upward, waiting on the crumbs that the government throws your way. This does not have to be the outlook of any black person in America today.

Of course it does not mean that life is not sometimes unfair. It does not mean that things will always work out our way. It does not guarantee success. The sad, awful truth is that in life bad things sometimes happen (including racism) despite our best efforts. That's life!

That is no reason however to walk around with our heads down, and our shoulders slumped, feeling sorry for ourselves because…the white man, the system or any of the other excuses that black people often use as reasons for taking a defeatist approach to life. There is no reason to always be suspicious of our neighbors simply because their pigmentation may be lighter than our own.

Always remain alert as a person should. Self preservation intuition is a gift from God. Stop seeing yourself as the hunted. There is no reason for it. Say no to the race pimps. Wave buh bye to the color hustlers, and reject the ethnoagitators. Tell Al Sharpton, Eric Michael Dyson, Mark Lamont Hill, Charlamagne tha god, and Ibram X Kendi to take their message elsewhere.

Black people are nothing but pawns in a sordid game of chess for white liberals like Joe Biden, Pete Buttigiege, Robert Francis O'Rourke, Elizabeth Warren and Bernie Sanders. These white liberals want nothing more than for black people to see themselves as poor defenseless victims. Each of them wants to project himself as the savior of Black Americans. In each of these politicians' twisted world view, black people need them to survive. Black people are incapable of thriving on their own without them. They fear nothing more than a black man or woman with a perspective outside of the status quo.

Black people do not have to follow the route that these hoaxers demand. Deal with adversity when it comes your way. Confront injustice as you encounter it. Fight for your rights when necessary, but as black people in America we do not have to view every shadow as a racist gun.

Let us, as black people, live as free beings with God on our side, charting our own course with guidance from above.

Recognize and Break Free Black People

The anti-police sentiment that now exists among some people in the country has been cultivated over a period of decades by politicians wanting to win the black vote. After being on the wrong side of every civil rights movement in the country's history, these politicians embarked on an insidious plan to sway the black vote to their side.

After the civil rights act of 1964 was finally passed, politicians who opposed the legislation began to tell black people nothing had changed. They began to tell them they should now look to said politicians for salvation. Despite all of the progress that blacks have made in so many different fields, and the many obstacles that they have overcome, these politicians have advanced a narrative that black people are victims of white America.

Today we have a black female Vice President. Just a few years ago we had a black President, not to mention other prominent black leaders who have held some of the most powerful positions in government. Black people are well represented in the public sector. Black General Officers have climbed to the highest positions of power in the Military. In addition, black people all across academia are in positions of influence. There are many successful black businessmen. People fill arenas all across America to see black people who dominate the major sports leagues.

In America, black people have access to numerous programs meant to help them advance their station in life. There are government agencies like the Equal Employment Opportunity Commission. This agency works to ensure employers do not discriminate against black people in the workforce. The Government aggressively goes after businesses that engage in discriminatory practices. Big businesses like Denny's, Texaco, Abercrombie and Fitch, and others know firsthand the consequences of allowing discrimination in the workplace. Businesses all across America have strict codes that serve to prevent discrimination in the workplace, and workers receive ongoing training to ensure that those they employ follow these codes. Interracial marriages are not uncommon and lynching is a thing of the past.

In the face of so much evidence, many now claim that the same level of discrimination still exists today...but it is more subtle. It is more insidious and it is disguised they say. They offer no proof of racism. All of their claims seem to be based on some innate ability they possess which allows them to read what is in people's minds, and to determine motivation. They are unable to point to concrete evidence of racism so they now talk about dog whistles and racist undertones. Every place there is disproportionate outcomes between blacks and whites is automatically attributed to race.

They love to speak of racist tropes where it is all up to them to interpret what someone said. Every bad experience that a black person has is now deemed to be discriminatory. Every

misfortune is reflexively blamed on white hatred. Every attempt
to wean people off the government teat to a life of independence
is said to be racist.

People must no longer be silent. The political party that has
pursued this strategy of division for the last five and a half
decades must now be called out. This is because their race
hustle has crossed a line. Their demagoguery is now literally
costing lives. Since the victories of the civil rights movement,
and the advances that have been made in race relations, it is the
same political party that has continued to insist things have not
changed.

The time has come for black people to seriously reassess and
reconsider their political alignment to the Democrat Party. As
black people continue to be told that the system is against them,
these same politicians continue to be in charge of the major
cities where chronic problems like crime, unemployment,
failing schools, and poverty are highest.

Cities like Baltimore, Ferguson, Chicago, Detroit and other
inner cities with these chronic problems have not seen changes
in their political structures for decades. These cities are all run
by the same political party that continues to blame the shadowy
system for the problems that many of their constituents face.

It is no wonder that today, despite all of the progress that has
taken place, the country is experiencing the most strained race
relations in decades. The pandering of these politicians has led

to a tragic turn of events which have led to the targeting of police officers. What is particularly disturbing is that a lot of the divisive rhetoric is coming from the highest levels of power. These people continue to push the false narrative. They refuse to allow the nation to heal because it serves their purpose to pit people against each other.

It is time for people (especially black people) to rebuff these politicians, and the political party that has continued to thrive for so many years off of the division they have created. The incessant drumbeat and constant appeal to race has become a cancer on the nation. It has metastasized and if we fail to recognize the cause of it we will continue to be captives to its sinister spread.

Black people, it is time to break free of these taskmasters! We can do better. Look around and take a good look at who has been running your cities. It is not the people that you continue to blame. Like parasites, these politicians are sucking away the life force of so many black communities, but for some reason black people continue to look to them for respite.

No political party has all of the answers to the problems that ail us. It is by the grace of God and putting our trust in him that we will know true success, however; It is our solemn duty to ensure that those we give stewardship over our affairs are the people who truly have our best interests at heart.

Chapter 5

Victimology 101

The Status Symbol Of Victimhood

B eing a victim in America has become a status symbol that people seem to hold on to for dear life. They guard it jealously. There are so many groups who claim to be oppressed by "the system" that it is difficult to keep up with their numbers. There is almost a paradoxical type of affluence to being a victim, and the subjects wear their perceived affront as a badge of honor.

They walk into a room and they feel that all eyes are on them as the (fill in the blank)-American who is always persecuted just for "being who he/she is." With this warped status symbol comes an attitude of expectation, and an outlook that they deserve special attention.

These "victims" see themselves as outsiders who are constantly targeted, and they refuse to believe that they have a fair shot at success. Many of them do not embrace the idea that they are full-fledged Americans unless they can get the power of big government on their side.

By viewing themselves this way, many often refuse to give the effort necessary to be successful. They find themselves as the main subjects in a series of self-fulfilling prophecies. Without providing any proof, and often referring to some anecdotal "evidence," they blame all or most of their problems on others discriminating against them because they are (fill in the blank) – American. This then becomes a badge of honor to them. This is like a soldier garbed in his dress uniform, proudly displaying all of the insignia he has earned over the years.

This embrace of victimhood comes with its "benefits" because others often take up the cause of the victim class and project themselves as their saviors. This recognition by sometimes very prominent people then gives legitimacy to different movements that further continue to keep people in a state where they always have to look to someone else to come to their rescue. Their rescuers are often willing to do whatever it takes to ensure their perpetual support.

This attitude is dangerous because of the inertia or militant behavior that it often engenders. The victim class justifies their lack of ambition and effort, or their combativeness by blaming "the system". They soon begin to demand rights that are not like the natural or God given rights guaranteed in the constitution (the right to speak one's mind, religious freedom, defend oneself, be secure in one's home, the right to your property, etc.). Instead many of the rights that they demand imposes on others and/or involves the distribution of "stuff" from the government largesse.

The following quote gives a look into the soul of the victim class, it reads "*In claiming the status of victim* and by assigning all blame to others, a person can achieve moral superiority while simultaneously disowning any responsibility for one's behavior and its outcome. The victims 'merely' seek justice and fairness. If they become violent, it is only as a last resort, in self-defense."

The victim stance is a powerful one. "The victim is always morally right, never responsible nor accountable, and forever entitled to sympathy." In their minds every difficulty they face is someone else's fault. They believe that they should be exempt from the natural consequences of living, and they strive all out to ensure that their ever increasing demands are imposed on the rest of society.

America was built on the idea of hard work and self-reliance. People understood that the life they lived was directly related to the extent of the effort that they gave. They also understood that life is sometimes unfair and things can turn awry. They understood that every bad thing that happens is not always because of some ubiquitous oppressor. Sometimes it's just life. There is real injustice in the world, there are real problems that we must address and aggressively tackle head on.

Americans have always confronted the clear, legitimate causes and injustices worth fighting for. They will continue to do so, and we are a much better society because of it. However, too many have latched on to the coattails of these legitimate causes to promote all kinds of dubious causes that promote the victim class, and/or divide the country. People have to be willing to stand up and fight this dangerous behavior or continue to see it gain more and more ground.

The Black Lives Matter Scam

The Black Lives Matter movement is one of the biggest frauds ever perpetrated anywhere in the world! It is not that black lives do not matter. Surely they do! In the eyes of God every life is precious.

There is no dispute that black lives matter. What is so offensive about the movement is not the statement in itself that black lives matter. It is the idea that black lives are undervalued and unappreciated in America. Therefore, we have to walk around sounding a trumpet repeating the phrase over and over again because...whitey, or the system or whatever the complaint of the day may be.

Black lives matter is a false alarm that needlessly implicates a whole bunch of people who hold no animosity towards black people as a group. Are there racists? Sure there are racists. One would have to be a fool to say there are no racists, but there are also sociopaths in the world. There are greedy people. There are malcontents in the world. There are people who love violence. In other words there are all kinds of evil in the world. People do bad for many different reasons. However when it comes to racism, liberals, leftists and Democrats magnify it like it is the biggest problem in America.

The truth is that we will always have racism, just like we will have all of the other evils that exist in a fallen world. This is until Jesus Christ comes again to make all things new. In the mean time however, wherever racism shows it's unsightly head we should deal with it, and fight it valiantly. However, the idea that racism is one of the biggest problems in America affecting the black man is a lie. It is based on a successful decades old propaganda campaign that has been waged to keep black people in a state of grievance. It is one of the most evil propaganda campaigns that has ever been waged.

Look at the damage it has wrought!

The more we as a country implement policies to make this a more just society, the more people complain about how terrible the country is. One day people will look back in history and shake their heads at how ungrateful twenty first century Americans were. Black lives matter agitators demand a utopian society before they can be grateful for what they have. Every day they are always looking for opportunities to be offended, and blaming every single bad thing that happens in their lives on racism and white supremacy. It is as though there is no other reason why bad things happen to black people

The black lives matter crowd are in hog heaven when they get the opportunity to point their finger at a negative experience they can blame on racism. They bask in the victimhood that ensues, constantly referencing various straw men as proof of their racism narrative.

 Never has their ever been a people so privileged, yet so ungrateful and happy to portray themselves as victims, as the black lives matter crowd. While they do this, they ignore the real problems, which, if they give attention to them, would go a very long way to improve the lives of black people in America. The black lives matter crowd refuses to do that though. In their sick world, being a victim is more to be desired. They are quite happy to walk around dragging those chains with a negative outlook on life.

Could anyone imagine if all of that negative energy was used to uplift black people? What kind of effect would there be on the black collective psyche if we were not telling them every single day that every shadow is a racist bogeyman?

How would the lives of black people improve if they did not walk around convinced that the average police officer whose job it is to protect and serve is out to do them harm? What if, as black people we concentrated on all the positive changes to correct past injustices that have occurred over the years?

How would it affect the lives of black people if every morning they woke up thinking that with God on their side anything is possible for them in this country that offers them so much? Instead it is just a constant negative barrage of woe is me because I am black. I am a second class citizen because I am black. I am disadvantaged and starting 17 paces behind everyone because I am black. The white man is privileged and I am not because I am black, and on, and on, and on, and on, and on, and on, and on, and....

As a people are we not tired of living this way?

Why would anyone want to continue living their lives in this manner?

Jussie Smullet And Victimology In The Black Community

Jussie Smollet has been found guilty on five charges relating to one of the biggest hate crime hoaxes in the country. More that two years after perpetrating it, he is still running the scam. Even after being found guilty he insists that he was a target of the racist hate crime as they call it.

Recently Ray Charles reached out from beyond the crypt to enlighten us. Ray wanted everyone to know that even though he is both blind and dead, he could see from where he is that something did not seem right with the whole matter. Ray said that if people were willing to remove their blinders, they too could have realized that there was more to the story. As the saying goes "none is so blind as he who will not see."

That seems to be the default position of the left and the Democrat party. They are willingly blind to the reality of life in this country. They are emotionally invested in the idea that America is a cesspool of racist hatred. Instead of simply battling racism where it does show its ugly head, and then keep on moving, they jump for joy because they get a situation to exploit. The Jussie Smullet story proved it again.

So by now we know that there was a lot more to the story than Mr. Smullet had us initially believe. The story quickly began to unravel after he first made the claim, and the sordid details were all over the news. Now to be truthful, who knows!?! It is

possible for a black man to be the victim of a hate crime in
Chicago. Keep in mind though that in Chicago, 88 percent of
the people voted against Donald Trump.

It is not impossible that he would be attacked by two white
supremacists shouting "this is MAGA country," in the middle
of a city that is predominantly black…with a large gay
population…where virtually no one voted for Trump…at two in
the morning…in the freezing temperatures of a polar
vortex…after waking up to have a snack and realizing that he
had nothing to eat at his place…then heading out in the freezing
cold…where he was beaten and rubbed. Whew! It is possible
but unlikely. Ok, let's get back to the point.

The point is that if this incident happened exactly as Smullet
claims it did, it still would not prove that white supremacy is a
major problem in the country. The reality is that white
supremacists are not running roughshod across America. The
Klu Klux Klan is not a group that has any influence in America.
The handful of Nazis in America are not power players socially,
politically, economically or otherwise. They hold no sway. If
they hold a rally, no more than a handful are represented. They
are always outnumbered tenfold by counter protesters who wish
to make it very clear to them that their vision for America is not
wanted or welcomed.

Displays, accusations, or the slightest hint of racism is the
fastest way to get people ostracized in American society today.
Businesses, educational institutions, and other organizations are

always putting systems in place to ensure that they aggressively tackle racism. There is a whole branch of government that is committed to fighting racism in the workplace, people can file individual lawsuits, and class action suits are common.

Many times businesses are willing to just settle lawsuits if they are accused of racism. HR departments across the country work hard to ensure that people are treated fairly on the job, but none of these things matter, or is enough for the race pimps in the Democrat Party, and on the radical left to accept that the system is not rigged against black people. They'd rather take incidents like what allegedly happened to Smullet, and gleefully hold it up as an exhibit of America's resentment of black people.

It is sad because the United States remains so needlessly divided on race, based on lies propagated by a handful of power hungry people whose modus operandi is to divide and conquer. Jussie Smullet should be a case study in victimology. Here is a young, handsome, successful black man with the world at his feet, but that was not enough for him. He longs to be a victim.

When asked why he thinks he was attacked, he said with a wry smile on his face in the most sanctimonious voice he could muster, "I really go hard at 45." Please!

He is just another prominent black man who has fallen into the trap, into which so many black people have fallen. They display an eagerness to trample around in the mire of victimhood, and want to invite as many people as possible to join them.

In addition, too many white guilt ridden liberals continue to promote the idea that black people are victims of white America. They have this need to present themselves as woke heroes of the black man.

These white liberals who want desperately to assuage their guilt ridden consciences for the evils of generations past, and show the world that they are the good whites have a big role to play in this unfortunate saga. They need to stop! Leave black people alone if that is the only way they think that they can offer their help to the black community.

Meghan Markle the victim, Harry the white hero

Hey y'all!

Meghan Markle is a victim y'all.

Whaaat! You didn't know? Whitey just wants to bring her down, and keep her in her rightful place. That place is underneath their privileged white feet. It is the only place for a black like her you see.

Did you see the Meghan Markle, Prince Harry interview? It played out just the way it was supposed to be played from the perspective here...the helpless black victim supported and encouraged by the caring white hero who wants the world to know he understands the plight of the black victim

The hype over the interview had all of the signs of what it was going to be all about, victim posturing and race pimping. All of the indicators suggested that this was going to be nothing more than a whine fest by a privileged one percenter beautiful black woman who is invested in proving, and showing the world that she too is a victim of the eeeeevil white devils. Next to her would be her rich, privileged one percenter, white husband, invested in proving to the world that he understands the plight of the poor helpless blacks (this is what they think of black people, and too many black people see it as a virtue in them).

The white dude understands how evil his people are, but he...he is one of the good ones. He has virtue doggone it! He wants the world to know. You see he is able to separate himself from the other white tormentors, and call it like it is.

Go ahead everybody, round of applause for Prince Harry. Go ahead, praise him, white savior that he is.

What better way to promulgate their race hysteria than having the ultimate one percenter, race baiting, black female invested in pushing the narrative do the interview? Who better to guide these two fools along than the grand old dame of race baiting herself? The one, the only, the indefatigable race baiting champyooon, Oprah Winfrey. You just knew what it was going to be. Each of them would just feed off each other and produce TV gold. As a collective, they would push the narrative that black people, who are highlighted in the travails of the lovely Duchess, cannot seem to get a break.

Initial thoughts were that the interview would just be a platform for Ms. Markle to spout that no one has ever had it as hard as she. This is all because she is black. People were mean to her you see, and that can only be because she is black. People need to understand that. Not even her husband's mother, Princess Diana, had it as hard as she.

Despite all of Markle's beauty, prestige, accomplishments and stature, she is just a poor black woman, hated for her skin color. Oh the distress of being poor old black Megsy.

True to form and as expected, Meghan and her white victim
enabler, cheered on by the race baiting black female one
percenter, flung out charges of racism. They provided
absolutely nothing to back up their highly charged accusations.
Hey! Who cares? Proof of racism against black people is never
necessary. As long as you feel it, it is. So there! The only reason
misfortune ever happens to black people is because of racism.

In the meantime many black people from all around the world
just lapped it all up, without an ounce of curiosity.

Why in heaven's name would any group of people choose to
live with such a defeatist approach to life? Why especially
would black people who have so much to gain by abandoning
this foolish way of thinking, and casting it into the garbage heap
of history?

Truth be told, there is racism in the world, but people are also
mean to black people for other reasons (by the way, racism is
not exclusively committed by white toward black people,
despite what you may hear). In some cases, it is because the
people being mean are just jerks. Occasionally, they are stupid.
Then again, maybe they are be having a bad day. They could
just be insensitive or ignorant. Other times they say things to
hurt because they feel hurt. Sometimes the person to whom they
are being mean is the jerk, or just unlikeable, or for other
reasons. In addition not every act of racism needs to be treated
like a national emergency. Sometimes it just needs to be waved
off like you wave off the nasty clerk at the DMV office. Other

times you deal with it like you dealt with the dude who tried to cut in front of the line at the grocery store.

The thing is people do not have to retreat into the victim posture every single time something bad happens to them. It's called life. Bad things happen from time to time.

In the end all the suspicions of what that interview would be about were spot on.

Nailed it!

The Consequences Of Encouraging the Grievance Culture

Ever seen the <u>video</u> of black residents in New York throwing water and flinging buckets at the police while the police attempted to do their duty? Then there was the video of black people jumping on top of a police vehicle and twerking as officers sat in the vehicle.

Since the death of George Floyd there have been numerous similar incidents targeting police officers. In some instances, crowds have even violently attacked the police for no other reason than being police.

This is what happens when the grievance culture is encouraged, when black people are constantly told that people are out to get them. When black people are told constantly that white people are a bunch of racists, they feel justified to behave this way because after all they are "victims".

When the same political party, decade after decade continues to tell black people that nothing has changed since the passage of the civil rights bills, and consistently hold black people to a different standard, this is what happens. From mostly black kids, and some irresponsible adults targeting white people in the "knock out game," to marauding black kids in malls, and other public places randomly attacking white people, this sort of behavior is never called out with the same type of fervor that we saw in Charlotteville.

More white people die at the hands of black people than black people die at the hands of white people, but that does not matter because liberals/leftists are always standing by to cuddle black people, and tell them that they "understand," though they do not condone the violence.

Universities now have on boarding classes exclusively for black students, separate dorms for blacks, they have courses in "white privilege." It is now acceptable behavior by university professors, sports media personalities, journalists and commentators to constantly attack the white male, and say things that would cause an uproar if said about a black person by a white person.

The restoration of the black family would go a long way helping to stop this madness. This has nothing to do with police brutality. That is just an excuse to continue propagating the victim culture and it has to stop. When we continually refuse to look inward, when we fail to do any self-examination, but instead point at all of the made up demons as the cause of the problems in the black community, this stuff will never end.

Black fathers need to be role models for their children. Education must play a more prominent role in the communities where these things consistently happen. People have to stop making excuses for bad behavior and hold these members of the black community to a higher standard. Teach them to respect the police and stress to them the importance of complying with the directives of the police when they have an encounter with them. This is what is needed.

The main reason that the police have so many negative clashes with black people is because black people account for 52 percent of all murders in the country. In addition, they account for 67 percent of all violent crime in these inner cities. Things will go wrong when there are so many negative interactions between the police and members of the black community.

This does not mean that there are no bad police or racist cops, but they are not the main problem. When they are caught in corruption, abusing their power or behaving in a manner that dishonors their profession they should be prosecuted. Let us however honestly confront the problems that exist in the black communities and start applying solutions to change the destiny of the next generation.

All is not lost, because not all black men buy into the narrative that they are victims. Not every black man is walking around enchained in a psychological prison of his own making. There are many black men who are not in captivity on the grievance plantation. There are many black people who do not walk around every day believing that the system is out to get them. They are free. They have to give young black men a positive message of hope, and help them to see that they do not have to succumb to the victim culture.

This is maddening!

Let us fix it with the help of God. It is not going to happen overnight, but it is possible over time if we address the problems honestly.

Chapter 6

Playing Blacks

The Democrats And Their Age Old Favorite Tactic

In 2020 before the elections, everyone knew that the Democrat machine was about to pull out their tried and true tactic. We all knew that the race card was about to come out and get played like they are at a poker tournament. After all, President Trump made inroads into minority groups unlike any other Republican president in decades.

Trump refused to pander to black people in particular, and he simply shook it off when the entire apparatus came against him and called him racist. He was not going to be defined by how the media defined him. Among the black citizens whom he had won over, they loved him for it.

Finally, here was a politician who did not just go into the fetal position, thumb in mouth, lying in a corner on the floor, rocking back and forth, crying and begging his accusers to stop calling him racist.

Trump simply did not care and it was epic. He quite simply ignored the race hustlers, the pimps, and the dealers. It was fascinating to witness, but everyone knew the evil Democrat machine was about to turn up the heat. What would they come up with next?

Candace Owens kept saying to look out because they will be coming with a vengeance. She said they are about to play the race card like we have never seen. Boy was she right! We knew it was about to happen, but no one was prepared for what came next.

The evil Democrat machine, aided by the complicit media, and all the hooligans on the left, found their opportunity in the unfortunate death of George Floyd. Unconcerned by the horrific terrible situation, all they saw was blood, and like true predators they went in for the kill. They exploited this man's death like a farmer exploits his land after discovering black gold on it.

These evil people were just ecstatic. Whaaaat! A black man died at the hands of the police under awful circumstances? What...what!?! Wohooo! This is it. This is it. This is what we've been waiting on all year long cried the evil Democrat Machine. They took the death of this man and played it like skilled fiddlers. It was music to their evil ears, and their mindless followers just danced to the hypnotic sounds produced by their instruments of deceit.

Many of the usual suspects showed up to celebrate...the Sharptons, the Obamas, the Dysons , etc. They did not just celebrate. No sir! They had a paaaarrrrrrtyyy! Of course many of the black people who have participated in these rituals in the past, were ready to play along. Like sheep being prodded by a shepherd's rod, they were just happy to be guided along.

Many of them led by their white liberal masters and the black field drivers proceeded to rampage through the streets of Democrat run cities, looting, burning, and running amok.

It was morbidly fascinating to behold as so many black people pretended to be oppressed. Just like George Floyd, they know what it's like to suffer under the knee of the oppressive system. They too are the persecuted.

They have no interest in the overall 70,000 black people who have been violently killed in the last 10 years. They just care about the handful of controversial cases involving the police. Big picture be damned. Data be damned. Information be damned. Circumstances be damned. Facts be damned. Anything that goes against the narrative be damned.

Feelings, feelings, feelings, raw emotions that work up people from the inside mean everything. The only thing that matters is portraying America as a racist cesspool where the system is shoving the faces of black people into the cesspool. As long as that is the image they get to portray they are doing well.

Since George Floyd, every black man shot or killed by the police has been used as a rallying cry to loot, burn, vandalize and kill. The irony is that the people shouting the loudest about racism are the people running the very cities they claim are racist. They are in charge and have been for decades.

This continues to be lost on the useful idiots who mindlessly follow these people, without ever exercising an ounce of intellectual curiosity. They have willingly put aside their capacity to think.

The people that make up the Democrat Party machine in the meantime are slapping their knees and thighs, holding their stomachs, swinging their heads back, and guffawing that once again; the race card has been their Trump card.

Gets 'em every time!

Well played evil ones…well played (slow clap).

Graveyard Celebrations

It happened again! Did you miss it? Black Lives Matter were dancing on the graves of a couple black men killed in other horrible circumstances by the police. BLM was rejoicing because they got to point their finger and use the terrible situations as "proof" that their lying narrative is true. America hates the black man they shouted with ecstatic glee. The police are out there targeting black men for no other reason than the color of these black men's skin. That is the only reason!

One more time let's do a hop, skip, and a dance over the misfortune that these black men suffered at the hands of the police. High fives everyone. Woohoo!

That is the theme of the Black Lives Matter movement. These people don't give a hoot about black people.

Once again, over 7000 black people are slain each year. Less than 150 of them are unarmed and killed by the police. Keep in mind that unarmed does not mean "undangerous." Many of these black citizens find themselves in hostile, aggressive situations with the police and end up getting killed because of their own actions.

No one is saying that's a positive thing. No one denies that it is heartbreaking. No one is saying we should not seek to find remedies to these situations. In fact no one even claims that the police are always blameless. In some of these situations the police perhaps could have handled the situations differently, but come on; can we at least be honest about all of this?

Yes, black men are dying at too high a rate by homicide, but the police are not the reason for this. Can we at least acknowledge this and stop the nonsense every time a black man is killed in an unfortunate situation like we saw in the George Floyd case? Just stop it!

One thing that can be done is to stop helping create the us vs them mentality in the interactions black men have with the police. If the police are seen as the enemy then that is already a problematic start when these interactions do occur.

How about promoting the idea that black fathers matter? That might be an even better place to start.

Democrats May As Well Tell Black People that Blacks are Stupid

Democrats are literally telling black people that having to show an ID card in order to vote is racist.

The reason that it is racist is because requesting an ID card to vote will negatively affect mostly black people. In other words, what the Democrat Party machine is saying is that black people are so stupid, so incapable, so utterly foolish and incompetent, that they can't figure out how to procure an ID card to vote.

That two year period between congressional elections, and that four year period between Presidential elections is just not enough time for black people to figure out how to get an ID card. First time voters and people who lose whatever ID cards they do have leading up to elections will not be able to figure it out either. They are just to dumb!

Black people just do not know how to make their way to get a driver's license, a state ID, or any other kind of official ID card, Neither do black people know how to use their social security card as identification.

Democrats believe that these same black people can figure out how to procure an ID card to buy liquor, cigarettes, open a bank account, attend the Democrat Party National Convention, get married, apply for welfare, apply for unemployment, get a job, etc. But oooooh! When it comes to that voting stuff, black people do not know how to get an ID card to do that. That's heavy intellectual stuff. Blacks can't handle it.

Black people do not know how to do that and they need Democrat politicians to swoop in and protect them.

This is what the Democrat Party thinks of black people.

Reparations, Another Democrat Scam

Do Democrat politicians believe there is any reason to love their country? These people are unbelievable! When was the last time anyone ever heard a Democrat politician speak a message of hope? That is not a rhetorical question by the way.

The Democrats seem to never have anything good to say about America. It is a constant barrage of negativity from these people without ever acknowledging all that is good and wonderful about this place. Listening to them, one would think that we are living in some kind of dystopian nightmare.

These demagogues who by their actions have demonstrated time and time again, that they could not care less about black people, held hearings on reparations. Can you believe this nonsense? Reparations…reparations? You have got to be kidding.

It is needless to say that slavery was an awful thing. It is a terrible stain on the country. We can all acknowledge that but my gosh! Slavery was an accepted practice in the world at the time. However, there were always people who were against it. In America in particular, it was always a cause of contention. The history of the world is of people and nations conquering, ruling, and dominating other nations and people. The victors always set the rules. That is simply the world that existed then.

How in heaven's name do we look at a country like America today though, and hold all of this bitterness for a practice that has so long been abolished? We are the only country that fought a war over slavery. It is true that even after slavery black people continued to suffer many injustices. But each step of the way, there were always people speaking out against injustice. They fought for a country that truly lived up to the ideal that all men are created equal and endowed by their creator with certain inalienable rights.

Slavery was a system that was deeply entrenched in America. It is a natural consequence that even after granting slaves their freedom, it would require even more work to change attitudes toward black people. That is what the country did. The nation did the work that was necessary to give us the country that we have today.

Instead of being grateful that we live in a country that took on the evil of slavery in a time when slavery was a common practice around the world, today we have the Democrat Party doing what they do best and stirring up grievance among its citizens over it.

Keep in mind that today in America, most people of European descent currently living in America have absolutely no connection to slavery in any way. They are not the descendants of slave owners. Here's the thing, even if they were, they should not be made to feel guilty about something in which they played no active role.

We should never forget the awful parts of our history. When we do, we are very likely to repeat the mistakes of the past. For crying out loud though! Can we stop looking behind, complaining about this issue as though we can do something about the past? Who gets to decide how far back in the past we should go anyway? Why not go back to the African countries where black people were selling other black people to the Europeans who were engaged in the trading of human beings? Should we be demanding payment from these African countries today? Why do they get a pass?

Folks, the past is past! The America that exists today is a place of opportunity for every citizen, especially black Americans. America has already done the hard lifting to correct injustices of the past. The people who continue to complain about every slight faced by black people today, whether these slights are real or imagined, will never be satisfied. This is because in their world perfection is the only standard that they will accept. Until every last sliver of injustice is eliminated they will not be satisfied. That is a fantasy. That utopian society does not exist anywhere.

It is true that we can never be satisfied, and we should always seek to do better no matter how good we have it, but can we at least acknowledge how good we have it and be grateful for that?

America has paid its dues, black people living in this country are not owed a single penny for slavery. There are so many systems and programs in place that black people can take advantage of to better their lives right here and now.

This whole idea of reparations only serves to keep the wounds over slavery that should have healed a long time ago festering. No one should doubt the desire of the Democrat Party to keep the country in a state of division. They thrive on selling the idea that black people are victims in America. That way Democrat politicians can always portray themselves as heroes coming to the rescue of these helpless black people who simply cannot make it without their Democrat benefactors.

Ladies and gentlemen this talk of reparations is a scam. It is a hoax that is meant to distract from the real issues that are facing people of every stripe in this country. Don't fall for it.

The Sad Truth about Abortion and Black America

20 million black babies never got to even see the light of day, that's twenty million since Roe vs Wade.

Like so many issues that negatively affect black people, this is perhaps one of the most insidious policies pushed by Democrat politicians.

In the meantime, since the carnage of so many black babies in the womb, the black population has stagnated. Planned Parenthood has flooded black neighborhoods with their clinics of death.

Black women, despite being such a small percent of women, account for about 35 percent of all abortions. We know that controlling the growth of the black population was the original intent of Margaret Sanger and Planned Parenthood. Thus far, they have succeeded beyond her wildest expectations.

Today as the black population hovers around 14 percent, the population of illegal aliens has exploded, creating a demographic change that has greatly affected blacks in this country. The changes that are taking place have a particularly negative effect on black Americans.

There is absolutely nothing wrong with a demographic shift that occurs naturally. It appears though that much of the displacement in the black community has occurred through abortion and illegal immigration.

Once again, as in the case with so many of the destructive policies that have been pushed in this country's history, the Democrat Party is at the forefront. They are leading the charge.

Chapter 7

Miscellaneous

Visitors from the Past

Imagine if Frederick Douglass, Booker T. Washington, Sojourner Truth, Harriet Tubman and other black freedom fighters, civil rights leaders and educators from the past were to somehow transmit themselves into twenty first Century America.

Let your imagination wander and picture it. They were informed about Barrack Obama, Colin Powell, Clarence Thomas, Condoleezza Rice, Eric Holder, Loretta Lynch and other black Americans who are in, or have been in positions of power and influence all across the country. They find out about the major cities that are dominated and run by black Americans and they can't believe it.

They look at the military where blacks are respected and have an equal chance of climbing the Military ranks. It brings a smile to their faces. Imagine their surprise when these honorable people find out that a black four star general was recently in charge of the U.S. Military and international forces in the strategic contingency theater of Korea.

In addition to all of this, they learn about affirmative action, and all of the programs that many well intentioned politicians and others have put in place to help lift black people out of poverty, to move blacks forward.

As these historical stalwarts of freedom continue to learn about the modern world, they learn about Brown vs Board of education. They learn that the KKK has been decimated and neutered. They learn that the KKK holds no political sway in the country. Everyone of them is pleased to know that even though white supremacy still exists, whenever white supremacist bigots attempt to have a rally or some public display of their evil ideology, they are always outnumbered by protesters at least ten to one.

Our group of visitors are delighted when they discover that lynchings are a thing of the past, and the Civil Rights Acts were passed decades ago. It brings delight to their hearts when they realize all of the laws that are in place to protect the rights of all citizens. They find out that the government and businesses can, has, and are often sued for racial discrimination. Human Resources departments all across the country have rigid anti-discrimination rules in place, not only to deal with discrimination when it happens, but to avoid it from happening in the first place. Everywhere diversity programs are in place to create an atmosphere of tolerance.

This noble group from our past then finds out about zero tolerance policies and they are truly impressed. While surfing the internet they find out that one of the easiest ways for a white person to be shamed and ostracized is to be labeled as a racist. In this regard they read about people like Paula Dean and Rosanne Barr, George Allen and others who are now treated as castaways because of their perceived racism.

As these accomplished black leaders continue on their modern sojourn, they continue to be enlightened about life in current day America. Each passing moment, they are more and more astonished. They simply cannot believe that black people can travel anywhere they choose, or live anywhere they wish.

They become overwhelmed with what they see. They are in shock when they learn about business moguls like Oprah Winfrey, Bob Johnson, Michael Jordan and successful businessmen like Herman Cain.

Now completely flabbergasted by all that they have seen, they find out about major sports leagues like the NBA, NFL and even the MLB that are dominated by black people and other minorities. Upon further inquiry they learn out about Serena Williams, Tiger Woods, Simone Biles and others. They just cannot get over all of the opportunities that black people have to improve their lives, and they stop to take in all in. It's a bit much but they'll be ok.

As they try to absorb it all, along comes Al Sharpton, Michael Eric Dyson, Kamala Harris, and other black victocrats with their white liberal enablers to enlighten these black champions. These victocrats and their white liberal enablers' sole purpose is to let these giants know that they should not get it twisted and be confused by all of these deceitful signs of progress. Black people are still suffering at the hands of the white man in America. The whole system is geared to keep the black man subjugated Messieurs Sharpton et al. try to convince our delegation of heros from the past.

Beto O'Rourke emphasizes to them that the system is unjust as it ever was for black people in America. He brings along Colin Kaepernick to help him reinforce the point. In the ensuing few hours Kamala, Al and company proceed to give our distinguished guests from the past all the examples that show what a horrible nation present day America is because there are evil people in the country, and bad things sometimes happen to black people.

With morbid delight, and an enthusiasm to rival a prospector during the California gold rush, these charlatans reference George Floyd, Jacob Blake and the handful of controversial shootings in the last year or two to show how unjust America is to the black man.

What do you suppose the response of Mr. Douglass, Mr. Washington, Ms Tubman, Ms. Truth and the whole group of heroes would be?

South Africa Under Apartheid Today, What If...

Imagine that the year is 2022. By some strange twist of faith and events, Nelson Mandela is still in prison in South Africa. The Government of South Africa is still brutally and systematically oppressing the black citizens of South Africa. The only reason for this subjugation of the people is because they are black. That's it!

Somewhere along the line though, the world decided that economic and political sanctions against the South African government were actually counter productive for the people. The reasoning is that by opening South Africa's economy to trade with the rest of the world, and ceasing to isolate them in other ways, it would lead to more political freedom, and less human rights abuses as the country begins to prosper.

Eventually the people of South Africa will be free because the country cannot realize its full potential if all of the people cannot fully participate as free citizens. Sounds good in theory, but with each passing year the world watches as the situation grows worse for the people of South Africa. The world turns a blind eye as the white South African government becomes more savage, and the black citizens of South Africa continue to live in fear of their government.

In the midst of all of this, there has been some economic mobility for the people despite the oppression. The South African government gains prominence in the world. Multinational corporations and conglomerates are reaping the economic benefits of an open South Africa. Many of these businesses have become rich beyond measure as a result. Their fortunes, to a significant extent are directly linked to South Africa, especially American companies.

As South Africa has continued to gain influence around the globe and they become richer, it seems as though the world has forgotten the original reasons for opening up the country to trade and other activities. In the meantime, Nelson Mandela is still in jail, and there is not one inch of movement toward a free South Africa for all of the people. Apartheid continues to be their political system, and in fact, the Government has continued to grow even more oppressive.

Although generally speaking, the lives of many black South Africans have definitely improved, they are still lagging behind the rest of the world by several miles. There is still a significant number of the population who are suffering economically. Though there is more hope to climb out of poverty, and there is reason for a positive outlook where that is concerned, the people know that their government still does not tolerate political dissent. Opponents of the government are still beaten, tortured, thrown in prison, and sometimes killed. Organs are harvested, and rape is used as an act of intimidation by the government. The families of political opponents are targeted and made to suffer for the actions of their relatives who dare to oppose the oppressive South African regime.

One day something happens. Another Soweto youth uprising occurs just like in 1976, because the people are fed up of being oppressed, despite the economic improvement in their lives. They want freedom.

Unfortunately though, just like in 1976, the authorities respond just as violently to the uprising. The people continue to protest nevertheless. Their actions led to a revival of the freedom movement.With each passing day, the government's response to the movement grows harsher.

Somewhere across the world, in a show of solidarity with the black population of South Africa, a guy by the name of Daryl Morey, a general manager of the Houston Rockets basketball team in the NBA sends out a tweet. The tweet ignites the ire of the white racist South African Government. The government then threatens the NBA with retaliation for allowing the Houston Rockets general manager to criticize their oppressive racist government.

The star player of the Houston Rockets even apologizes to the South African Government for his boss's tweet supporting the oppressed people of South Africa. Many people are shocked and outraged by the NBA kowtowing to the South African Government who is telling Americans what they are allowed to say in their own country.

On another occasion in a different interview, one NBA owner is asked about the black citizens suffering under the hands of the South African Government. The owner replies "Nobody cares about what's happening to black people in South Africa, OK? You bring it up because you really care, and I think it's nice that you care. The rest of us don't care. I'm just telling you a very hard, ugly truth. Of all the things that I care about, yes, it is below my line."

Everyone then turns to the NBA's social justice warrior extraordinaire to get a response. They are disappointed because he too refused to support the people of South Africa, suffering under the thumb of their oppressive government. Instead the king of social justice warriors in the sports world talks about how the tweet had the potential to jeopardize people financially and in other ways.

Dissatisfied with that answer from the guy who knows how to speak truth to power, the people press him further. Finally he says "I'd be cheating my teammates by continuing to harp on something that won't benefit us trying to win a championship because that's what we're here for," he concludes "We're not politicians." In other words, he's just going to shut up and dribble.

Well…this is all a hypothetical scenario, but can you imagine it?

The White Supremacy Threat

Society should call out with a loud voice and identify white supremacy for the evil that it is. They should do it like they do for any other evil ideology. It is unacceptable! It must be condemned wherever it rears its ugly head, whenever it rears it's ugly head.

That said, let's be honest. The idea that white supremacy is a problem that is pervading American society is a ruse. It is ridiculous! One more time, this is not to say that racism does not exist. It surely does. One would have to be a fool to make such a statement. In a country as large as the United States of America, that is as diverse as America, it is impossible for there not to be racism. The idea that white supremacy is a major threat to American society however is a tool that is used by politicians. It is used to scare people into voting for certain politicians, and turn away from others. It is a weapon meant to drive discontent, keep people divided and send them retreating into different camps.

For a large segment of the population, people do not have to actually do racist things in order to be considered racist. One simply needs to have certain political beliefs, and that is enough for others to label that individual as a racist. It is a sinister tactic that is part of an overall strategy designed to keep citizens' minds off of real issues, and instead focus on the white supremacist bogeyman. When you are constantly chasing the monster in the shadows, you do not notice the intruder coming through the window.

The race hysteria has kicked in to overdrive since Trump but it's been running for a long time. Here are some examples of how it works. When Bush was in power Charlie Rangel, a former black Congressman from New York once said, "It's not spic or nigger anymore, Republicans just say cut taxes." When Obama was at the helm, one media commentator once said "Republicans are using the IRS scandal as their latest weapon in the war against the black man. 'IRS' is the new 'nigger.'"

Did you get that? Look at the racist monster over here. Forget the real issue of the IRS abusing its power by targeting opponents of the administration.

These are examples of what the corrupt media and their leftist allies now reference to show racism. The tactic works. For many, when these crooks labeled opponents as racists, the conversation then shifted from tax cuts, and a really huge scandal that involved the IRS, to making sure that the "scary evil racists" don't attain, or are removed from power.

During the reign of Barrack the great, this tactic of labeling every political disagreement as racist also went into high gear. Every criticism or mean word spoken against the great one was labeled as racist. Just the fact that his holiness was black and most of his detractors were white was sufficient grounds for his political opponents, or people who simply did not like him to be called racist. It went like that for eight straight years. If you opposed Obamacare you were a racist who did not like that a black man was in charge, etc.

If people make a case for voter ID laws, they were immediately called racist, and the topic of voter integrity laws shifts. After all, everyone knows racist laws are bad, right?

Over the years the bar to label someone as racist has been lowered to such an extent that the most skilled limbo performer could not get under it. Racist acts are no longer required to show racism. No proof is ever necessary! The only thing needed is the assurance in the accuser's mind that the accused is racist.

This glib use of the word racism is only ever directed against one group…white people, and it does not matter how much improvement there continues to be in race relations. The charge of racism will be hurled at anyone without hesitation despite how a person has lived his or her entire life. One slip of the tongue is all it takes, and an individual's reputation, career and life could be ruined by the charge of racism.

In America today a person could recover from being labeled a psychopathic murderer faster than being labeled a racist, yet the refrain continues. The beat of the drum is constant. America is racist. White supremacy is a major threat in America. It is a lie! It is a crafty device that is meant to shade certain people and policies from criticism. The constant cries of racism are meant to scare political opponents into silence, and to destroy them if they dare open their mouths.

Many white people walk around on eggshells, scared to death of being stigmatized as racist. They fold up into the foetal position cowering in the corner at the mere idea of being branded a racist. Many of them try to deflect negative attention by joining the chorus, and condemning others as racist for no sound reason.

These white saboteurs then get to brag about "telling it like it is," or "speaking truth to power," when in fact all they are doing is signaling their own virtue. In the process they continue to tear the country apart based on a completely false narrative.

Again, just to be completely clear, no one here is saying that racism does not exist. News flash! We will always have racism, just like we will always have other forms of evil.

The way to deal with racism is to identify it, confront it where and whenever it shows up, then keep on moving. The idea that racism and white supremacy is woven into the American fabric is laughable.

More people should stop being afraid to say so and treat it for the joke that it is.

Blacks, Hard Work And Sports Entertainment

Think about all of the black athletes who dominate the major league sports in America. Even in many of the sports that black people do not traditionally play, we have seen black athletes come to dominate them. It is a testament to the hard work that they put in to be successful at their chosen endeavor.

Tiger Woods rose to dominate the world of golf and in doing so inspired other young black boys to get involved in the sport. The Williams sisters ascended to the top of the tennis world. They too have inspired many young black girls and boys to get involved in the sport, and achieve success. Bubba Wallace worked hard and he broke through to become a favorite driver in Nascar.

Most of the super stars in the NBA are black. The league is about 75 percent black even though blacks make up about 14 percent of the American population. Lebron James has mastered his craft and reaps the benefits of his dedication. The top quarterback in the NFL just signed the first half a billion dollar contract in the world of sport. He is a black man and one heck of a football player. His skill and dedication were rewarded.

To make it in the world of sport and earn a living doing it is extremely difficult. It requires a lot of hard work, dedication, talent, and timing. It is really, really difficult to make it in the world of sport.

For many young black men, they see sports as the only way to make it out of their difficult circumstances. Though the percentage of people who earn their living playing sports is very low, of the number who do, the percentage of black people is quite significant.

They are successful because they put in the hours to harness their skills. They make the sacrifices necessary to improve their skills. They put in the long hours of practice. They spent countless hours practicing free throws, throwing the football, hitting the baseball, running the tracks, doing whatever it takes to be successful. When clubs see the value that these dedicated men and women can add to their organizations, these clubs do not hesitate to make them a part of their teams. Color does not matter because of what they bring to the organization.

The Los Angeles Lakers is a valued franchise because of the long list of talented players who have been a part of their organization. This includes a larger number of black players. Lebron James is the top basketball player in the world. His sheer presence on the Los Lakers, together with a group of other really talented players make the team's games must-see exhibitions.

Nobody cares that so many of the players on the team are black. When people come to see them play, the fans just want to see great basketball. Lebron James, his top compeer Anthony Davis, and the rest of their cohorts seldom fail to deliver.

They have dedicated themselves to their craft. They have put in the grueling work to get where they are, and have earned all of the rewards that they reap. Because they are so skilled at what they do, many other opportunities have automatically opened up to them. They now traverse worlds that otherwise they may not have known. They are reaping what they have sown.

Now with all of the talk that we hear about how terrible and hard it is for black people to make it in America, imagine a world in which many young black people demonstrated the same dedication to becoming engineers, doctors, lawyers, scientists, computer programmers, teachers, entrepreneurs, public servants and other professionals.

Would these black people not have the same measure of success, and the opportunities that come in their chosen fields of endeavor? Or does America hate black people so much that the only place black people can be successful is in the field of entertainment where they fit a certain stereotype?

Hate Crime Hoaxes

As <u>hate crime hoaxes</u> go, Jussie Smollet's was one of the most high profile, but his fraud was not just an aberration. Hate crime hoaxes are more common than one would think. They have been happening for years, and for the most part they have been moving in one direction. When was the last time anyone saw a hate crime of conservatives falsely blaming lefties for an attack? Not saying it has not occurred, just asking. Where are the reports? That is because when things are really happening on such a large scale the way that conservatives, and anyone supporting Trump have been attacked, there really is no need to make up stories about it.

It is mostly people on the left who make up these false stories in the attempt to portray the white hatred ruse. With the election of Donald Trump, hoax hate claims increased exponentially. From the muslim woman in "Louisiana who claimed in November 2016 that two white men, one of whom was wearing a Trump hat, attacked and robbed her, taking her wallet and hijab while yelling racial slurs," to the black church member who was responsible for setting his own church on fire, they were all hoaxes.

The media never spent even a fraction of the time they spent promoting the hoaxes as they spent exposing them. Then there was the lefty journalist, Juan Thompson, who alone was responsible for scores of calls threatening to firebomb synagogues. He wanted to make Trump supporters look like rotten bigots. A 19-year-old Jewish man who is an Israeli-American dual citizen was arrested for similar crimes. Police believe the man made over 120 fake bomb threats in New Zealand and Australia and against scores of Jewish institutions across the U.S.

Imagine if Fox News, Newsmax, The Daily Caller, Newsbusters, the Daily Wire, Breitbart, The Gateway Pundit, and other alternative media did not exist! All of these would have been swept under the rug.

These are people so desperate to paint America into the image that they want people to believe it is, that they have literally engaged in hundreds of hoaxes or acts of vandalism, then tried to palm it off on Trump supporters or conservatives in general. If it is as bad as the left would have us believe then there would be no need to perpetrate all of these hoaxes.

It is so terrible, that the grand poobah of all hoaxers gained notoriety and fame after perpetrating one of the biggest hoaxes in American history. His name is Al Sharpton, anti-semite premier. He is a giant in the Democrat Party. This man's history is there for anyone to examine, but it does not matter.

He has never apologized for any of his histrionics, including one incident in which seven people ended up dead. On the left, he is a star with a show of his own. That is how empowering it is to be a Democrat, especially a black Democrat.

Again, this fraudster gained national recognition based on a lie about a young black woman called Tawanna Brawley. Go read about it for yourself, and while you are at it; check out his role in the Crown Heights riot. The man is a bunco artist, but a beloved bunco artist, never held to account.

The following is a list of hoaxes, and fake news that have been perpetrated going back to just a few years ago up to the present. Many of them are less than a year old. This is just a sample to remind people of what we are dealing with when it comes to this issue.

Here is just a handful of fake news and hate hoaxes designed to frame political opponents as rabid racists:

Spokane, Washington, middle school ordered black students to "pick cotton" as a school assignment: HOAX

Racist frat party at East Carolina University invite sent out and said 'No blacks:' HOAX

Noose found in Connecticut HS restroom: HOAX

Rockies fan called black player nigger: FAKE NEWS

Bubba Wallace noose: HOAX

A few years ago prosecutors charged a LGBT activist with burning down her own home with pets inside. MAJOR HOAX.

Jussie Smollet attacked by two MAGA wearing white Trump supporters: Gargantuan HOAX!

White Covington Catholic kids staged racist attack on Native American elder: FAKE NEWS!

Black seven year old girl shot by white assailant in drive-by shooting: FAKE NEWS!

Pittsburgh synagogue shooter is a Trump supporter. FAKE NEWS, (the guy actually despised Trump).

Drake University student receives racist notes: HOAX!

On Goucher college someone scrawled "KKK," swastikas and "I'm gonna kill all niggers" across Goucher College campus: HOAX!

A few years ago the South Carolina President of the NAACP (an NAACP official! Let that sink in) claimed he was racially profiled, and he complained about a climate of hate: HOAX!

Ciera Calhoun, a black nurse claimed she and her friends were racially profiled by the police. Police released body cam footage: HOAX!

How about the Long Island woman who claimed that four Trump supporters shouted "get out of the country" at her,

slashed her tires and left a hateful note on her car?
Nah…HOAX!

Here is another high profile one: a Waco restaurant waitress
claimed that a law enforcement officer scrawled a racial slur
against Hispanics on a receipt: HOAX!

In November of 2018, according to the Daily Caller "the
suspect in a synagogue vandalism act that forced the
cancellation of a Democratic event is reportedly a former City
Hall employee who worked on anti-hate crime issues, and is a
Democratic activist." Hoax!

There is no shortage of people who have been violently attacked
for the simple act of wearing a MAGA hat, but all we ever hear
about from the dishonest media is how hateful Trump's
supporters are.

To give an indication of how prevalent hate hoaxes are, there
are websites dedicated to tracking and recording them.

Always be suspicious of the hate crime reports with Joy Reid,
Don Lemon and the rest hyperventilating over them. Your
natural response should be to doubt it, then do your own
research to determine what the truth is and respond accordingly.

Racial Disparities In school Disciplinary Measures

There are serious racial disparities in disciplinary measures doled out to black and Hispanic students, and white and Asian students in schools across the country. Black and Hispanic students are three to four times more likely to be suspended than white and Asian students. So what do these figures mean? Is it because the system discriminates against black and Hispanic students? Of course Democrats say yes. Instead of investigating the issue to determine why there is such a large discrepancy between disciplining these groups, a few years ago, the Obama administration, led by the race baiting hustler Eric Holder, concluded that the only reason for it was...wait for it...racism!

So how did they respond to the discrepancy?

They initiated a policy urging more lenient forms of discipline for minority students, even for dangerous behavior. They claimed that leniency on bad behavior would benefit students because it would help them to avoid incarceration. Do you get that? It did not matter that black and Hispanic students were far more likely than white and Asian students to commit the kind of offenses that require school officials to summon the police, suspend the students, or implement other disciplinary measures against them. The most critical thing for Democrats was narrowing the gap, not reducing unacceptable behavior.

Now obviously helping students to avoid the pitfalls of unsociable behavior should be a priority for educators, but when the focus moves to avoiding discipline in order to avoid the consequences of bad behavior, something is obviously wrong. These misguided policies always have a way of swinging around to bite everyone in their...um...posterior. That is what seems to be happening around the country and New York in particular.

One Democrat senator in New York and a teamster President is complaining that the stupid Obama policy has led to a "lack of accountability for dangerous behavior." Like with so many dangerous Democrat leftist policies, that even people with the cranial capacity of a dodo bird could see, this one also was bound to have unintended consequences. The policy did manage to reduce the disparity in disciplinary measures between black and Hispanic students, and white and Asian students. However, that came with a cost that many teachers, students, parents and others are not willing to pay.

According to CBS news who spoke to NY State Senator Leroy Comrie "parents are taking their children to other schools even if they have to pay for private schools," said Comrie. He went on to say "They don't want to have their children in an environment where they're assaulted and there's no accountability." As the good people say, yuh think?

Teamsters President Gregory Floyd, who represents school safety officers also spoke on the issue. "There's chaos in our schools and it's going to get worse," he said. "The children know they can get away with everything." The CBS report went on "the softening of discipline began with a DeBlasio administration policy started several years ago that issued warning cards instead of criminal summonses. Parents should be outraged," Floyd said. "They should be horrified and outraged."

So once again what we have here is the soft bigotry of low expectations when it comes to the way white leftists treat black people. Instead of holding black people to the same standards as everyone else, white liberals hold them to a lower standard and think that they are doing blacks a favor. In their minds blacks can't do better so they need white lefties to be their heroes. In the quest to assuage their white guilt, they institute all kinds of silly rules that only help to take black people backwards.

This awful policy aimed at reducing incarceration rates does nothing to help black people. By telling them it is the system and not their own behavior that is responsible for the discrepancy in discipline that is meted out to black students, it means that black students will not see the need to address the real issues at hand. As bad behavior goes without repercussions because of this dreadful policy, it may in fact serve to help increase incarceration rates. Consequences be damned!

The "good intentions" of white liberals and pandering Democrats are all that matter. As long as they get to feel good about themselves, it does not matter that blacks and Hispanics are the ones who will reap those negative consequences.

Cultural Appropriation?

If there was ever a doubt that many black Americans bask in the status of victimhood, the evidence is seen in a new trendy complaint. Many now complain about so called "cultural appropriation." All over campuses and other places in America, young black activists confront white Americans about white people "stealing their culture." The people who engage in this behavior that feeds off of a victim mentality do it with gusto. With the same fervor of a pig rolling around in a smelly sty, they roll around in the sludge of victimhood.

They see themselves as special because they are victims, and they seize every opportunity to promote the narrative that they are. They refuse to thrive. This should give an idea of how crazy it is. One of the higher profile people who was targeted as a perpetrator of abuse by members of the victim brigade a couple years ago is a singer by the name of Justin Bieber.

What was Mr. Bieber's crime, you may ask? Get ready for it because it is egregious. Mr. Bieber dared to (wait for it) "appropriate" dreadlocks as a hairstyle. The audacity of this white man! What creative way will these people find to continue humiliating and oppressing black people? As the sound of the violin continues, let us step back, take a look at this nonsense and call it out for the utter foolishness that it is.

Instead of seeing themselves as trendsetters, as Americans leading the way in the style league, many black Americans whine about others taking "their culture". This attitude driven by white leftists is indicative of the mindset that many of them have consciously chosen to adopt. They see themselves as some type of "other," and not as real Americans. They stand on the outside and refuse to engage as Americans. They do not view themselves as contributors in the context of the larger American culture, but instead to "black culture." They view this as a very distinct and separate culture. It has no place in any concept of a unified people. In this context, R&B is not American music but black music, rap is not an American art form, it's a black thing, white people wearing dreadlocks are not copying a fad popular with Americans, but they are copying a black fad.

If a trend, type of music or practice is considered to be the exclusive domain of black people, then conversely, the same holds true for white people, Asian Americans, Hispanics, etc. It would then mean that no black person should ever aspire to the opera, being a ballerina would be off limits to people of color because it is not "their culture"? Practicing martial arts like Kung Fu and Karate would not be practiced by anyone outside of the Asian culture according to this reasoning. We can even take this silly rationale further by questioning whether a person of Chinese decent would have any business learning Karate, or whether a person of Japanese origin should practice Kung Fu, because like other ethnic groups; Asians are not monolithic, and they do have different cultural practices.

Some practices may have cultural roots in a particular group, but that does not make the practice the exclusive domain of the group, because in a cosmopolitan society; cultures often become intertwined and developed into their own customs to form a unique common culture.

Sure there are some practices that are unique and sacred to distinct groups, and there are times purely out of respect to these groups, in these unique circumstances that society defers to them and their traditions, but those are rare instances.

The drivel that is being promoted by members of the victim posse on the other hand is something that must be rejected by clear minded people, because to endorse it is to give it legitimacy that it does not deserve. Not because a trend, a style, type of music or anything else was started by a black person or any other group for that matter, does it mean that it is black culture or the culture of the other group.

Again, if we were to consistently apply this principle, it would further mean that a black person has no right trying to make it in Nascar, a Hispanic person would not be allowed to open a Chinese restaurant, and a person of Asian descent who may love the Quinceañera tradition and wish to incorporate aspects of it into their own traditions are committing a "cultural crime". We should embrace the unifying of a people (the American people) in this manner, but instead we use it to continue promoting the "us versus them" syndrome.

People are either woefully unaware or they do not care that this behavior promotes the segmentation of society, and discourages unity among the people. This philosophy when encouraged and pursued leads to the Balkanization of nations because it rejects the notion of a common culture (an American culture in this instance). This may seem farfetched. However, it is important to remember that many of the radical changes that occur in societies do not happen overnight, but over a long period of time. Radical ideas are implemented slowly, and little by little.

Eventually people become numb to the changes. Over time and with each new generation, radical ideas seem like the norm.

Reject the radicals of all stripes.

The NFL Clown Show

"The Black National Anthem!" Are you kidding, are you kidding…are you kidding?

The NFL has become, and continues to be a clown show. It is now a place where liberal politics has a home, and a place for social justice warriors to thrive. This clown show has regularly featured rich, privileged, spoiled black men earning millions of dollars to run up and down a field chasing a ball, telling Americans what an awful country America is.

Life is great for the clowns of the NFL. They will readily admit that personally they are not victims. They do however want to give voice to the millions and millions of black people across the land who they do view as victims of the evil system in place. The system is designed for no other reason than to make the lives of black men miserable.

These clowns consider themselves to be brave for standing up to "the man." Their politics matter as much as their football skills. When they stick their middle fingers in the faces of their fans they show how selfless they are, because after all, "It is not just about football." These clowns are "woke" and they want the world to know that they are woke.

They deceptively view themselves in the same light as Tommie Smith and John Carlos who gave the famous Black Panther salute during the 1968 Olympic Games. They are convinced that their grand standing is on par with other great civil rights athletes of the past who truly had cause to protest. As far as these clowns are concerned, their cause is no different than the cause of their predecessors who fought for a fairer America.

As these clowns take over the entire circus, the ringmasters look on in admiration. Instead of taking control back from the clowns, they encourage the farce. As clowns usually do, the clowns of the NFL rely strictly on emotion to spread their message. With these clowns it is no laughing matter though, because at the end of their act, the only things they evoke are feelings of grievance and anger.

They have absolutely no data to back up any of their sensational claims, only anecdotal "evidence," and other incidents that often contradict their narrative. These clowns have no interest in the epidemic of violence that exists in the black community.

As a handful of black men slaughter other black men by the thousands every year in their communities, these clowns remain silent. They only care about the handful of black men who die at the hands of the police in controversial circumstances.

The clowns of the NFL are not interested in protesting the many absent fathers in the black community, the high rate of children born out of wedlock, or the high school drop out rate. They continue to point to "the disproportionate numbers of black men in prison" as proof of persecution.

In the minds of these NFL clowns it is not possible that black men are jailed in disproportionate numbers because they commit crime in disproportionate numbers. It must be the white man's fault. It is the white man's system that's guilty. To demonstrate how brave they are, and to fight the power they began to trample under foot one of the few remaining symbols that Americans use as a demonstration of solidarity to reflect on what is good about the country. Now they are playing the "black national anthem." Whatever that is!

What is wrong with these people?

Well done NFL clowns!

UTOPIA!

In a land far away there is a place where many leftists and Democrats can finally find true happiness and contentment. In this land, unicorns roam freely in lush fields of orchids. As they roam, they sprinkle magic petals, and leave trails of miracle dust that continue to make everything alright. In this land there is no competition for anything, no visible opposition on any issue, and everyone agrees on every point. The people are all beautiful and everyone's a winner there!

No one is judged for personal behavior. There are no consequences for the decisions people make or the acts they commit. There are no grievances, no injustice, no war, no racism no crime and everyone is equal.

Best of all there are no police officers. No effort is required to make one's dreams come true, or to achieve one's goals. No one wants for anything, there are no obstacles to overcome. Nothing terrible ever happens there.

In this idyllic place Colin Kaepernick was seen mysteriously standing with his hand on his heart, paying tribute to what sounded like the American national anthem.

About The Author

The author is from Trinidad and Tobago, the most southerly of the Caribbean, West Indian archipelago, nine miles off the coast of Venezuela from the closest point. Like so many immigrants who have come to the United States, he understands how blessed he is to live here in the America.

He migrated over 26 years ago and says that his life was never the same from the first day that he set his feet on American soil. He says he was blown away by the sheer grandeur of the place, and utterly amazed that so much opportunities to be successful existed for anyone who was willing to put in the work.

For a poor, uneducated immigrant who prior to arriving in America, was never able to make much progress in his life, America was everything that he thought it would be.

He has a Master of Science in Administration degree, a Bachelor of Arts degree in Organizational Management, has worked for the U.S. Government and has written some articles for a prominent government organization.

The author has always been taken aback by the hatred that so many Americans have for their own country. The explosion of noxious anti American sentiments by American citizens continues to baffle him.

The constant appeal to race and the incessant effort to paint the country as a downright evil nation that has contributed nothing to the world, and has made no progress since the days of slavery, often leaves him scratching his head. He quite frequently finds himself wondering if the minds of the complainers exist in an alternate universe while their bodies are simply refined zombie manifestations walking around the country.

He sometimes believes that one of these days, even after all of these years, he'll awaken to half of the country standing over his bed. Everyone will be peering at him. They'll then begin cackling loudly and uncontrollably, grabbing their stomachs, slapping their knees and thighs, flinging their heads back, pointing their fingers at him, and screaming "you've been punked."

References

60 Minutes interviews the prosecutors of Derek Chauvin. (n.d.).

Www.cbsnews.com. Retrieved December 9, 2021,

from *https://www.cbsnews.com/news/derek-chauvin-*

prosecutors-george-floyd-death-60-minutes-2021-04-

25/

A quote by Frederick Douglass. (n.d.). Www.goodreads.com.

Retrieved December 9, 2021, from

https://www.goodreads.com/quotes/802386-

everybody-has-asked-the-question-what-shall-we-do

Archive, V. A., Author, E. the, Twitter, F. on, & feed, G. author

R. (2016, July 12). *How Obama ruined his Dallas*

memorial speech. New York Post.

https://nypost.com/2016/07/12/how-obama-ruined-

his-dallas-memorial-speech/

Archive, V. A., & feed, G. author R. (2021, September 13). *Bill*

Maher: NFL's move to play "black national anthem"

is "segregation." New York Post.

https://nypost.com/2021/09/13/bill-maher-disagrees-

with-nfl-playing-black-national-anthem/

Berry, D. S. (2019, March 8). *Officials Point to "Chaos" in*

Schools Since Obama Discipline Policy. Breitbart.

https://www.breitbart.com/politics/2019/03/08/democ

rat-lawmaker-teamster-president-chaos-schools-since-

obama-era-discipline-policy-no-accountability-

dangerous-behavior/

Caplan, J. (2019, October 16). *LeBron James Refuses to*

Address China Backlash: "We're Not Politicians."

Breitbart.

https://www.breitbart.com/sports/2019/10/16/lebron-

james-refuses-to-address-china-backlash-were-not-

politicians/

CNN, F. K. (n.d.). *Justin Bieber is being accused of cultural*

appropriation over his hair. Again. CNN.

https://www.cnn.com/2021/04/27/entertainment/justin

-bieber-dreadlocks-trnd/index.html

Donald, H. M. (2020, July 3). *There is no epidemic of fatal*

police shootings against unarmed black Americans.

USA TODAY.

https://www.usatoday.com/story/opinion/2020/07/03/

police-black-killings-homicide-rates-race-injustice-

column/3235072001/

Dorman, S. (2021, January 22). *An estimated 62 million*

abortions have occurred since Roe v. Wade decision

in 1973. Fox News.

https://www.foxnews.com/politics/abortions-since-

roe-v-wade

Expanded Offense. (n.d.). FBI. https://ucr.fbi.gov/crime-in-the-

u.s/2019/crime-in-the-u.s.-2019/topic-

pages/expanded-offense

fakehatecrimes.org. (n.d.). Www.fakehatecrimes.org. Retrieved

December 9, 2021, from

https://www.fakehatecrimes.org/

Gaydos, Ryan. "Daryl Morey 'Very Comfortable' with Hong

Kong Tweet despite Immense Backlash." *Associated*

Press, 24 Dec. 2020, www.foxnews.com/sports/daryl-

morey-very-comfortable-hong-kong-tweet. Accessed

14 Dec. 2021.

Hadfield, J. (2020, July 30). *Barack Obama Uses John Lewis*

Eulogy For Political Diatribe, Attacks Trump. The

Political Insider.

https://thepoliticalinsider.com/barack-obama-uses-

john-lewis-eulogy-for-political-diatribe-attacks-

trump/

Huston, W. T. (2020, May 7). *LeBron James on Ahmaud Arbery Killing: "We're Literally Hunted Everyday."* Breitbart. https://www.breitbart.com/sports/2020/05/07/lebron-james-ahmaud-arbery-killing-were-literally-hunted-everyday/

Huston, W. T. (2021, July 9). *Study: NBA Commentators More Likely to Praise Light-Skinned Players, Criticize Dark-Skinned Players.* Breitbart. *https://www.breitbart.com/sports/2021/07/08/study-nba-commentators-more-likely-to-praise-light-skinned-players-criticize-dark-skinned-players/*

Jury acquits Tulsa officer Betty Shelby in death of Terence Crutcher. (n.d.). NBC News. Retrieved December 9,

2021, from *https://www.nbcnews.com/news/us-*

news/jury-acquits-tulsa-officer-shooting-death-

terence-crutcher-n761206

Karet, B. (n.d.). *Right-Wing Media Attack Obama's Eulogy For*

Fallen Dallas Police Officers As A "Middle Finger

To Cops." Media Matters for America. Retrieved

December 9, 2021, from

https://www.mediamatters.org/ben-shapiro/right-

wing-media-attack-obamas-eulogy-fallen-dallas-

police-officers-middle-finger-cops

LeBron James Responds to Laura Ingraham's "Shut Up and

Dribble" With Powerful Post About Police Brutality.

(n.d.). NBC Los Angeles.

https://www.nbclosangeles.com/news/sports/lebron-james-responds-to-laura-ingrahams-shut-up-and-

dribble-with-powerful-post-about-police-

brutality/2375333/

Michelle Obama Blames Black Voters for Trump's 2016 Win.

(2020, May 5). Newsmax.

https://www.newsmax.com/politics/michelle-obama-

netflix-becoming-2016-

election/2020/05/05/id/966090/

Minnesota, V. R. W. R. is an A. vet who lives in, Analyst, H. I.

a F. I., Owner, B., & roll, is an N. L. member who is

officially retired but has yet to slow his. (2019, July

7). *Michelle Obama: "I guess it's like, if the black*

guy can do it, anybody can do it ... that's not true. It's

a hard job." BizPac Review.

https://www.bizpacreview.com/2019/07/07/michelle-

obama-i-guess-its-like-if-the-black-guy-can-do-it-

anybody-can-do-it-thats-not-true-its-a-hard-job-

772313/

*MSNBC's Martin Bashir: "IRS" Is the New "N****r."* (2013,

June 5). National Review.

https://www.nationalreview.com/corner/msnbcs-

martin-bashir-irs-new-nr-charles-c-w-cooke/

Obama, race hustler extraordinaire, cheers punishing

Georgia's economy. (n.d.).

Www.americanthinker.com. Retrieved December 9,

2021, from

https://www.americanthinker.com/blog/2021/04/obam

a_race_hustler_extraordinaire_cheers_punishing_ge

orgias_economy.html

Progressives and Blacks. (2013, August 20). CNSNews.com.

https://www.cnsnews.com/commentary/walter-e-

williams/progressives-and-blacks

Psychology of Victimhood, Don't Blame the Victim, Article by

Ofer Zur, Ph.D. (2019, February 12). Zur Institute.

https://www.zurinstitute.com/victimhood/

RAW: Released George Floyd body cam footage from former

officers Thomas Lane and J. Alexander Kueng. (n.d.).

Www.youtube.com. Retrieved December 9, 2021,

from

https://www.youtube.com/watch?v=NjKjaCvXdf4&t=

41s

"Rockets' James Harden Apologizes for GM Daryl Morey's

Controversial Tweet about Hong

Kong." *CBSSports.com*,

www.cbssports.com/nba/news/rockets-james-harden-

apologizes-for-gm-daryl-moreys-controversial-tweet-

about-hong-kong/. Accessed 14 Dec. 2021.

Since Roe, abortion has killed more black babies than the entire

black population of the U.S. in 1960. (2020, February

28). Washington Examiner.

https://www.washingtonexaminer.com/opinion/op-

eds/since-roe-abortion-has-killed-more-black-babies-

than-the-entire-black-population-of-the-u-s-in-1960

Tash, D. (2020, July 3). *Higgins: Enough of the lying – just look*

at the data. There's no epidemic of racist police

officers killing black Americans. Citizens Journal.

https://www.citizensjournal.us/higgins-enough-of-the-lying-just-look-at-the-data-theres-no-epidemic-of-racist-police-officers-killing-black-americans/

The Battle for Iwo Jima. (n.d.).

https://www.nationalww2museum.org/sites/default/files/2020-02/iwo-jima-fact-sheet.pdf

Trump Once Again Falsely Linked The Black Lives Matter Movement To An Anti-Police Chant. (n.d.). BuzzFeed News. Retrieved December 9, 2021, from

https://www.buzzfeednews.com/article/tasneemnashrulla/trump-blm-chant-pigs-in-a-blanket-false-claim

(n.d.). *Video Shows NYC Protesters Chanting for "Dead Cops."* NBC New York.

https://www.nbcnewyork.com/news/local/eric-garner-manhattan-dead-cops-video-millions-march-protest/2015303/

Viral Videos of People Throwing Buckets of Water at NYPD Officers Sparks Outrage | NBC New York. (n.d.). Www.youtube.com. Retrieved December 9, 2021, from

https://www.youtube.com/watch?v=M0YmzNsQDDs

Ward, E. (2018, November 28). *CDC: 36% of Abortions Abort Black Babies.* CNSNews.com.

https://www.cnsnews.com/news/article/emily-ward/blacks-make-134-population-36-abortions

WHITE LUNACY on parade as woman refuses to see "Black Panther" movie for fear of "sucking the Black joy out of the theater"... HUH? (2018, February 15).

NaturalNews.com.

https://www.naturalnews.com/2018-02-15-woman-

refuses-to-see-black-panther-movie-for-fear-of-

sucking-the-black-joy-out-of-the-theater.html

Wilber, D. W. (n.d.). - *"Pigs in a Blanket, Fry 'em Like*

Bacon". Townhall. Retrieved December 9, 2021,

from

https://townhall.com/columnists/dwwilber/2015/09/02

/pigs-in-a-blanket-fry-em-like-bacon-n2046574

I'd love to know what your reading experience with this book has been. I'd be grateful to hear from you, and for you to tell me what you think. I encourage your feedback. Please leave a review. If you would like to say more, feel free to engage with me at the email below: Email: upoppolitics@gmail.com

Unpopular Politics
https://www.facebook.com/groups/435596161559668

Made in the USA
Monee, IL
24 March 2022